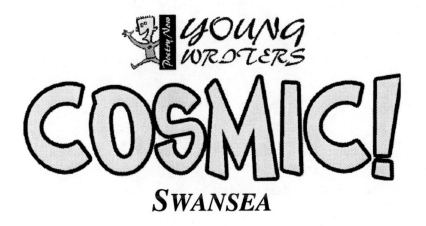

SWANSEA

Edited By Dave Thomas

First published in Great Britain in 1998 by
POETRY NOW YOUNG WRITERS
1-2 Wainman Road, Woodston,
Peterborough, PE2 7BU
Telephone (01733) 230748

HB ISBN 0 75430 038 2
SB ISBN 0 75430 039 0

FOREWORD

With over 63,000 entries for this year's Cosmic competition, it has proved to be our most demanding editing year to date.

We were, however, helped immensely by the fantastic standard of entries we received, and, on behalf of the Young Writers team, thank you.

The Cosmic series is a tremendous reflection on the writing abilities of 8-11 year old children, and the teachers who have encouraged them must take a great deal of credit.

We hope that you enjoy reading *Cosmic Swansea* and that you are impressed with the variety of poems and style with which they are written, giving an insight into the minds of young children and what they think about the world today.

CONTENTS

Ilona Svikeris   1

Blaen-Y-Maes Primary School
    Jamie Jones   1
    Leanne James, Kerry Morris
        & Melanie Evans   2
    Kevin Thomas   2
    Damion Evans   3
    Kayleigh Coffey   3
    Gemma Ivett   4
    William Baker   4
    Danielle Williams & Zoe Davies   5
    Michael Cooper   5
    Adrienne Jones   6
    Heather Hinton   7

Caehopkin CP School
    Alun Jenkins   7
    Christopher Williams   8
    Amy Hopton   8
    Keiron John Williams   9
    Lyndon Jones   10
    Andrew Williams   10
    Nathan Ace   11
    Jessica Ann Roberts   12

Cwmllynfell Primary School
    Timothy Davies   13
    Richard Oliver   14
    Emily Fyfield   14
    Kieran Bennett   15
    Aled Williams   16
    Zeke Davies   16
    Elin Kinsey   17

Gors Junior School

Rebecca Parry	18
Jenna Wright & Natalie	19
Hazel Barratt	19
Jennifer Ann Williams	20
James Gaylor	21
Emma Penfold	21
Lee Price	21
Ashley Rees	22
Gemma Anderson	22
Ashleigh Thomas	23
Nathan Wright	23
Holly Richards	24
Tracy Thomas	24
Kathy Howell	25
Alison Jones	25
Lucy Pickin	26
Richard Harris	26
Timothy Driscoll	27
Jay Lovell	27
Dafydd Press	27
Sarah Kervin	28
Matthew Thomas	28
Christopher Hookway	28

Mayhill Junior School

Kylie Evans	29
Lindsey Lerwell	29
Daniel Evans	30
Christopher Davies	30
Christopher Courtney	30
Gemma Underhill	31
Jenna Grove	31
Kimberley Martin	31
Jodie Ford	32

Oakleigh House School

Tennille Rees	32
Jane Vancura	33
Lucy Bassett	34
Sophie Batty	34
Flora McKay	35
Amy Ward	36
Holly Nicholas	37
Julia Heath-Davies	37
Rosanna Zorko	38
Louise Rowley	39
Alex Roberts	40
Jacqueline Bassett	41
Stephanie Wookey	42

Pengelli Primary School

Emilie Williams	43
Stephanie Thomson	44
Stuart Mindt	44
Owen James	45
Scott Thomas	45
Christina Evans	46
Mark Owens	46
Annie Lee	47
Sam Batsford	47
Christopher Hinchey	48
Kenneth Rees	49
James Evans	49
Jenna Pugh	50
David Morris	50
Scott Roberts	51
Cheryl Davies	51
Michelle Planck	52
Lewis Evans	53
Charlotte Thomas	54

St Joseph's Cathedral School

Jason Garrett	54
Laura Davies	55
Lauren Thomas	55
Angharad Fowler	56
James Morgan	57
Sean Voyle	57
Paul King	58
Jodie Boyes	58
Kirsty Evans	59
Siobhan Williams	60
Jason Trueman	61
Gabrielle Browne	61
Norena McCready	62
Ben Davies	62
Nicola Marsh	63
Jon-Paul Wayne-Morris	63
Charlotte Evans	64
Sarah Lloyd	64
Charlotte Rogers	65
Daniel Lacey	66
Alix Scrine	66
James Matthews	67
Adam Davies-Cross	68
Carys Evans	68
Thomas White	69
Michael Jones	70
Katie Burton	70
Laura Martin	71
Dean Harris	72
Maybelle Morris	72
Christina Charalambou	73
Saira Souliman	73
Elizabeth Collins	74
Laura Frost	74
Daniel Penman	75
Laura Martin	76
Scott Hart	76

Emma Carlsen	77
James Meade	77
Emma Thomas	78
Martin Goold	78
Sarah Martin	79
Nicholas Taylor	79
Sara Rainey	80
Bethan John	80
Sarah Powell	81
Scott Clark	81
Rory Oldroyd	82
Joanna Parsonage	82
Michelle Romano	83
Rebecca James	84
Daniel Jones	84
Christopher McCarley	85
Cathal O'Connor	86
Jessica Kennedy	86
Daniel Richards	87
Peter Hinder	88
Lee Boland	88
Liam Nolan	89
James Evans	89
James Steward	90
Carlie Norman	90
Nicholas Morris	91
Nicholas Stevens	92
Aaron Davies	92
Michael McGrotty	93
Natalie Davies	94
Samantha Ahern	94
Rebecca Donovan	95
Kurt Velardo	96
Joseph Parkhouse	96
Gary McMullen	97
Bethan Michelle Flavin	97

St Joseph's RC Primary School, Clydach

Freya Thobroe	98
Ffion Cooke	98
Juliette Harris	99
Gabrielle Barrett	99
Kurien Parel	100
Catherine Morgan	100
Erika Butler	101
Hayley Codd	102
Michaela Jones	102
Victoria Jones	103
Natalie Johnson	104
Gina Earland	105
Jennifer Lloyd	105
Fiona Ryan	106

Terrace Road Primary School, Swansea

Heather Tucker	107
Lucie Barron	108

Tre-Gwyr Junior School

Samantha Ace	109
Scott Daniel McCoubrey	110
Sarah Ace	110
Jonathan Lewis	111
Lucy Chieffo	112
Rebecca Johns	112
David King	113
Damion Williams	114
Amira Bond	114
Alyx Williams	115
Charlotte Miles	116
Rhian Bateman	116
Emma Thomas	117
Christopher Williams	118
Dawn Elizabeth Emmerton	118
Leigh Jago	119

Waunarlwydd Primary School
   Adam Vaughan   119
   Gavin Morgan   120
   Christopher Lazell   120
   Amy Ross   121
   Geraint Probert   121
   David Berry   122
   Sarah Miller   122
   Thomas Stephens   123

Ynystawe Primary School
   Sam Bevan   124
   Elizabeth Chambers   124
   Sam Barrett   125
   Delyth Morris   126

Ysgol Gymraeg Ynysgedwyn
   Jason Williams   126
   Catrin James   127
   Lowri Evans   128
   Alex Glendenning   129
   Holly Best   129
   Bethan Morgan   130

THE POEMS

THE IRON MAN

The iron man was smashing.
The iron man was crashing.
The iron man was bashing.
The iron man was crying.

Ilona Svikeris (8)

ALADDIN

Everyone is on,
Because it's panto time,
Wishy Washy is a dim wit,
And he messes up the rhyme,
Sarah Autton is Aladdin,
John Buckland is the genie.
Micheal Cooper is Ebeneezer,
And he is a real meanie,
There is Ebeneezer's gang,
And a princess,
She looks really nice,
In her brand new dress,
Sarah Autton is a lovely lass,
She is the spitting image of her dad.
Ebeneezer is a meanie,
He always tries to get the genie,
There are boys and girls of all ages,
Here upon the wooden stages.

Jamie Jones (11)
Blaen-Y-Maes Primary School

ALADDIN

Welcome to our concert
Rehearsals here and there
Mrs Denton sewing
For costumes throughout the year
Photocopier going mad
Making panto tickets for you and me
Our concert is waiting
For you to come and see.

Leanne James, Kerry Morris & Melanie Evans (11)
Blaen-Y-Maes Primary School

MY NEW TRAINERS

I've got a pair of trainers,
I wear them every day,
They're glistening, shining, gleaming,
Floppy, polished and snug.
Hear them shuffle down the street,
Hear them echo with a beat,
Feel them floppy, snug and warm,
Smell them polished like never before.
The tongue is short,
The upper hard,
When they move they make the noise plod.
They're my new pair of trainers can't you see,
They're glistening, shining and glittery.

Kevin Thomas (11)
Blaen-Y-Maes Primary School

THE RIVER NILE

Young
Really happy, river starting
Moving fast down the rocks
Slowly to the middle
Middle-age
Getting bigger as it goes
Getting tired as it moves
Getting older as it flows
Old
Really oozy, really tired
River miserable, creeping sadly
Getting sleepy as it's dying.

Damion Evans (8)
Blaen-Y-Maes Primary School

WINTER

Winter is a snowy day when you open the
fridge and you see it that way.
Snow is like a man that has painted the world.
Frost is like a freshly baked cake with
sugar sprinkled on top of it.
Fog is like a dusty cloud and when you
stand in it, it goes around.

Kayleigh Coffey (8)
Blaen-Y-Maes Primary School

SPANISH MONSTER

There once was a monster from Spain
Who was a real pain
He jumped off the bus
Oh what a fuss
He's landed head first down the drain.

Gemma Ivett (9)
Blaen-Y-Maes Primary School

POISONOUS POEMS

Put a spider down her skirt.
Horse manure and lots of dirt.
Millipede legs and scrambled eggs in our brew.
Make her drink it and she will spew.
Give me a squid from the sea.
Half the bone of a wombat's knee.
I want loads of earwigs.
Plenty of twigs.
Get a mixture of chocolate this minute
Right now.
Don't forget to give me a mad diseased cow.
We will boil it and mix it and make it go bang!
It will make her go fizz, like a cola can.

William Baker (10)
Blaen-Y-Maes Primary School

OUR POISONOUS MEDICINE

Give me an earwig.
The runt of a pig.
Give me a spider,
That will crawl inside her.
Give me a snail that cannot see,
Give me a squigler from the tree.
Give me some smoke
She'd probably fizz like a can of Coke.
Granny dear, don't speak.
Can you hear it creak, creak, creak.
Get some squigler from the sea,
Coconut juice from a ju jube tree.
Cut some coconut juice inside.
Granny, Granny, you've got a big surprise.
Granny, Granny I wish you knew
What I've got in store for you.

Danielle Williams (10) & Zoe Davies (9)
Blaen-Y-Maes Primary School

MY ZIP ZINGER TRAINERS

Hear the trainers plod on the floor,
See the glorious colours rushing by.
Feel the warmth of the floppy insoles,
Say goodbye as they echo home and
Zoom away from your hands.
So you notice you're wearing the same *zip*
Zinger trainers.

Michael Cooper (11)
Blaen-Y-Maes Primary School

THE NILE

Young
The river is born
Happy, splashing,
Sparkling, rolling,
Tumbling in and out of the mountains.

Middle-age
The river is getting red,
The river is silky smooth,
Soft, crinkling,
Swishes as it moves.

Old
The river is dying,
Oozing, creeping,
Feeling miserable as it moves,
The river gets really sleepy,
Goes very . . . very . . . slow
And then it
D . . . I . . . E . . . S.

Adrienne Jones (9)
Blaen-Y-Maes Primary School

FRIGHT

Monday night I had a fright
Right in the middle of the night
I saw a ghost by my door
With its teeth hanging out
It was ready to bite.
I screamed and cried
There was nowhere to hide
So I screamed and said 'Don't hurt me,
I'm just a little girl.'

Heather Hinton (11)
Blaen-Y-Maes Primary School

COSMIC

As I went up to see the stars,
I saw some flying cars on Mars,
Pluto was small like a football,
The sun is bright and that is right.

I saw a collision in the sky,
The planets were whizzing by,
I saw the moon with a big spoon,
I wish I could visit them soon.

Alun Jenkins (10)
Caehopkin CP School

COSMIC

The planets are coloured
and very round.
What would you do if
they hit the ground?

Earth is like a great
big ball.
What would happen
if it would fall?

The sun is bright and
that is right.
What would you do if it
was blue?

The stars are light and
that is right.
But what would you
think if they were pink?

Christopher Williams (9)
Caehopkin CP School

COSMIC

As I went out on my daily fly,
I saw an alien whizzing by,
It looked at me like a buzzing bee
It flew so fast I could not see.

I followed him up into space,
He called me up, it was a race,
I was winning but he whizzed so fast
I lost the race, I came last.

Amy Hopton (10)
Caehopkin CP School

COSMIC

Through my window I only see
a spaceship, some stars and Mercury.
We travel a mile and see the sun,
I want to get out and have some fun.

Jupiter is huge and Pluto is small,
I wish I could go and visit them all.
So many colours, what a great sight
but remember the sun with its powerful light.

The stars so hot and the moon so cold,
'You can't go there' I was told.
Well out I jumped into the sky,
my mother screamed as I floated by.

I drifted around the galaxy
it was so lonely with only me.
Down I flew onto Mars
it was different there, not like the stars.

Down I jumped back to Earth,
at last I was on my own piece of turf.
Watching TV on the settee
I wonder what I'll have for tea.

Keiron John Williams (10)
Caehopkin CP School

COSMIC

In the night stars are bright
shooting their light across
the sky.

Pluto is small but Jupiter is
big, Mars is red but Venus is pink.

Ships are scraping the ground
then two laughing aliens that
are really having fun.

Lyndon Jones (9)
Caehopkin CP School

COSMIC

I said 'Today's the day I go into space.'
Now I pack my bags and my suitcase,
I put in there my favourite bear.

I'm up in space with my huge suitcase,
I can see the whole galaxy,
And all the planets I'd like to see.

The sun is hot and Mercury too,
Uranus is green and Neptune blue.
Jupiter is tall and Pluto is small,
One day I'll be back to visit them all.

The voyager probes I can see,
There, up in space watching me,
It's time to go home for a nice cup of tea.

Andrew Williams (11)
Caehopkin CP School

COSMIC

As I was walking down the street,
I met an alien on his feet,
He wasn't flying in the sky,
He was on his scooter whizzing by.

Through the window I could see,
Uranus, Mars and a coloured TV,
I saw my bedroom floating by,
Higher and higher past the sky.

The moon called out 'Come and see,'
I wonder where he's taking me?
Then I saw a blinding light,
It was the sun shining bright.

I looked around,
Guess what I found?
It was an alien on the ground.

He stood tall with dark all around,
He didn't make a single sound.

'Hello,' I said and he said back,
'Could I have a Big Mac,
I only want a snack.'

He asked me to take him back to Earth,
And I asked him 'What is it worth?'

Nathan Ace (9)
Caehopkin CP School

COSMIC

I'm so alone, I'm up in space,
But the sparkly stars distract me.

I'm so alone, but I see,
Tiny balls of fire, shining at me.

I'm so alone, I hear crackling,
From the most amazing sight, the sun.

I'm so alone, red and gold,
Orange and black, a colourful sight.

I'm so alone, I watch the planets,
Jupiter the biggest planet catches my eye.

I'm so alone, but I can see,
Pluto and Mercury and Neptune, blue.

I feel so alone, but I can see,
Aliens like us, multicoloured and clawed.

I'm so alone, and I see,
Saturn, Uranus, and Venus, non identical.

I'm so alone, and I see,
Asteroids in a circle, whizzing by.

I'm so alone, and I see,
The orion and the North Star.

I'm so alone and I see,
The animals of the stars, the unicorn and lion.

I'm so alone, and I see,
Earth, so dull,
But I have to go back.

Jessica Ann Roberts (11)
Caehopkin CP School

NATURE

Trees rustle in the blank stillness of night,
And wake up in the morning flame of life
That is the sun.

Workaholic ants on six employed legs each,
Manufacture their own castle
Of rotting vegetation.

Lord of the jungle circles his enemies,
Outraged in an urge for meat.
Prowling like a bushfire,
Pierces his target like a spear,
Injecting the bite of death
Into his opponent.
He is the true warrior of the trees,
Always will be king.

The sky so high and mighty,
Giving rain to the thirsting ground.
It can punish its creatures
With flashes of light
Or blasts of thunder.
It settles.
Now it is time for the great circle of life
To rest behind the
Giants of the ground,
And for the sky to show its darkest secrets
And open its thousands of eyes.

Timothy Davies (11)
Cwmllynfell Primary School

SPACE

Comets glowing in the black velvet sky,
Amazing but dangerous.
Eating their way through the atmosphere.
Colourful stars and planets,
Circling the sun for energy and life.

Sensationally, people make unauthorised landings,
But still they discover new things to do.
Searching for water,
Wandering in the atmosphere for energy.

Colourful it is to look at,
It's like a funfair,
Throwing its light upon the earth.
Bright stars, like a saucepan, pointing the way,
The way to Bethlehem, where Jesus was born.

Richard Oliver (11)
Cwmllynfell Primary School

WOODS

Leaves whispering to each other,
Toadstools popping their heads out
Of the ground,
Elves singing and dancing,
Juicy blackberries ripening.

People who come in the summer,
Having picnics under
Huge branches.

Rabbits digging holes
For burrows,
Poisonous snakes,
Like foxes as they hunt.

Enormous trees,
Giants of the forest,
Acorns that grow into oaks,
Lords of the kingdom.

Emily Fyfield (10)
Cwmllynfell Primary School

CHRISTMAS

White feathers floating in the air so softly,
Mountains covered with a white carpet of snow,
Streets full of happiness,
And Christmas tree lights all aglow.

Bells jingle and sing so delightfully,
Shining like brand new stars,
Father Christmas flying with the birds,
Rudolph struggling as if he's come from Mars.

Everything's quiet, except the bells,
Presents laid out everywhere,
Amazing decorations on the tree,
Christmas is sensational after all,
Isn't it?

Kieran Bennett (11)
Cwmllynfell Primary School

OPENCAST

Gazing down at the enormous site
full of metal monsters,
and diggers eating
strata of black gold.

The huge Demag,
munching strongly into the black carpet,
eating 50 tonnes a minute,
making mincemeat out of the rock
as it breaks through,
its links spinning.
Enormous trucks bucking fiercely,
dropping their precious gold into heaps.
Back and forth they come for more.

4pm, time to go, engines off.
They have worked their best,
those yellow men all shining bright,
like bees, like fireflies,
home in the night.

Aled Williams (11)
Cwmllynfell Primary School

NATURE

Colourful plants blowing in the wind,
Beautiful butterflies floating like leaves,
Birds sailing and opening their wings.

Bears like rumbling thunder growl,
Blue skies so cloudless,
'Amazing nature!' I cry to the world.

Glorious sun, so bright and glowing,
Like hundreds of fireflies
Beaming down on all of us,
This yellow light.

Little ants making homes in
Nature's kingdom,
Spiders crawling around,
Eating flies and
Beetles too.
All this nature for me and you.

Zeke Davies (9)
Cwmllynfell Primary School

DAFFODIL

Lady daffodil,
nodding her yellow sun bonnet,
blowing her trumpet loudly
in the wind.

Leaves like children surrounding her,
waiting for their food
from the glittering sun.
Spring is here!

Attractive duchess, gleaming in the sun,
smiling beautifully,
curtsying up and down
at her royal children.

Elin Kinsey (11)
Cwmllynfell Primary School

MY DOG BONNIE

Bonnie the pup,
licks my cup.
She likes to eat meat,
and to chase our feet.
When she eats her food,
she's in a real bad mood.
She has black fur,
I really love her.
She's always drinking Mum's tea,
she's always chasing bumble bees.
Bonnie's quite a naughty pup,
she barks all night and wakes us up.
She's always licking at her paw,
she stretches her legs out on the floor.
She's got brown eyes,
she really likes meat pies.
She's always trying to give me a bite,
she's always watching me fly my kite.
She's really, really sweet and cute,
Bonnie really likes her blue skin suit.
She likes biting at my socks,
she likes playing in a cardboard box.
She likes watching our TV,
she gets in the way, then I can't see.
She's always, always sniffing about,
but she's very scared when she gets a shout.
She's often, often wagging her tail,
and she's doing it like she's a whale.
She's really grand in every way,
more than words could ever say.

Rebecca Parry (7)
Gors Junior School

MY DOG

I have a little dog, he's always in a mood.
He's always clever, the only thing he's not clever at
Is finding me and you.
He gets pocket money twice a week,
It's not much, but it's worth a treat.
His favourite treat is lots of bones,
He licks and chews, but then he groans
Because he's got a tummy ache,
From eating meat and too much steak.

Jenna Wright (9) & Natalie
Gors Junior School

MY DOG

My dog is fluffy and fun,
He lays in the garden under the sun.
I take him for a walk in the park,
But I'm not to take him after dark.
He wakes me up when I'm in bed,
But he won't go away until I pat his head.
He sleeps in his basket nice and snug,
And when he wakes up I give him a hug.
He eats dog food, meat and fish,
All from his blue plastic dish.
When I come home from school
The first thing I see is my dog and that's cool!

Hazel Barratt (10)
Gors Junior School

MY RABBIT

I have a rabbit
its name is Peter
who likes to sit
by the heater.
He's got long ears,
he's black and white,
he likes to watch me
fly a kite.
He's cute and cuddly,
sweet and soft,
his favourite place
is in the loft.
He likes to bite
a carrot top,
when he eats one
he can not stop.
My best friend says
he's the best,
she's got one like it
but he's a pest.
His favourite game
is hide and seek,
every game we play
I peek.
At night he's curled up
in a ball
by the heater
in the hall.
I would not swap him for another
neither would my little brother.

Jennifer Ann Williams (8)
Gors Junior School

MY DOG

I have a dog called Skip
he's a little rip
and if you don't play his way
he will give you a nip
that little rip called Skip.

James Gaylor (10)
Gors Junior School

SNOWMAN

One warm thick hat
One soft woolly scarf
Three hard black lumps of coal
One big fresh carrot
No snow!

Emma Penfold (11)
Gors Junior School

DISCO

Brand new clothes
Lots of energetic people
Big hall for dancing
No music.

Lee Price (10)
Gors Junior School

WHERE DIFFERENT PEOPLE LIVE

Some people live in tall houses,
Some people live in short houses.
Some people live in nice houses,
Some people live in horrid houses.
But some people don't mind where they live
As long as they're with their family.
Some people don't live in houses,
They live on the bare street
With nothing to eat,
With no family.

Ashley Rees (10)
Gors Junior School

TEACHERS

Teachers are there to help you
When you are stuck.
But you could do nice work with a
Bit of luck.
You play on the computer and do other things
You can even make turtle doves with lovely wings.
Most of the things are good
But some are boring.
But you don't hear people snoring.
I like my school
It's really cool
I like my teachers, they're really nice
But sometimes we have to sit like mice.

Gemma Anderson (10)
Gors Junior School

RECIPE FOR AN AUTUMN MORNING

Recipe for an autumn morning
Lazy sun in autumn time,
Now I see you gently shine,
Autumn time of coloured leaves,
Gold and red upon the trees,
Harvest fruit so good to eat
Crops of barley and of wheat.

Ashleigh Thomas (9)
Gors Junior School

MY DOG

My dog, my dog
I love
him to
bits but next
Christmas I'll
have a frog
I love my
dog, I love him to bits
but next Christmas I'll
have a frog.

Nathan Wright (7)
Gors Junior School

EXCITEMENT

My excitement is as yellow as hot,
runny honey.
It tastes like the tangy juice of
a ripe lemon.
It smells like a sugared almond
waiting to crack open.
My excitement looks like a blazing
hot fire, with wood crackling and
spitting.
And sounds like a Catherine
wheel twisting and turning or a
banger that's booming.
It feels like a bird cracking
out of its small, white eggshell.

Holly Richards (11)
Gors Junior School

CONFIDENCE

My confidence is green like the wavy grass,
It tastes exhilarating like fresh mint toothpaste,
It smells like a field full of clover on a summer day,
My confidence looks like a tower of iron.
It sounds like a warrior preparing for war.
My confidence feels strong and uplifting.

Tracy Thomas (10)
Gors Junior School

DEATH

My anger is as black as a graveyard,
It tastes like crushed, powdery black paint,
It smells like smoke from a burning fire,
My anger looks like the devil
Coming out from a black puff of smoke,
It sounds like a ghost train racing
Through the clouds on a stormy, thundery night,
It feels like the Grim Reaper
Breathing down your back.

Kathy Howell (10)
Gors Junior School

LOVE

My love is like an enormous red ruby
not for sale.
It tastes like a double chocolate
gateau.
It smells like a jar of honey freshly
opened this morning.
My love looks like flowers blooming
in spring.
It sounds like two love birds singing
to each other.
If feels like a ball of flaming hot fire.

Alison Jones (11)
Gors Junior School

LOVE

My love is the colour of a sun-ripened apple.
It tastes like candy sugared lips touching mine.
It smells like a freshly picked scented rose.
It looks like me and James on a moonlit dance floor.
And sounds like a wolf crying out for company in the moonlight.
It feels like a fragile newborn baby.

Lucy Pickin (11)
Gors Junior School

ANGER

My anger is red and like a dragon blowing
hot flames that suddenly turn into ashes.
It tastes like a sour tooth bleeding in a
wet mouth.
It smells like a fire burning in a tattered
village.
My anger looks like a big bear trampling
through the woods.
My anger sounds like an express train racing
down the tracks.
And feels like a chill running down my neck.

Richard Harris (9)
Gors Junior School

SUPERMARKET

New staff
Hungry customers
New freezers
Empty tills
Baskets and trolleys
No food!

Timothy Driscoll (10)
Gors Junior School

MY ANGER

My anger is as red as a star in its last days,
It tastes like burning hot chilli peppers.
It smells like warm polluted air.
My anger looks like a raging fire
Spitting and crackling
It sounds like bombs exploding.
And it feels like sharp jagged knives.

Jay Lovell (10)
Gors Junior School

ICE HOCKEY

Shining new blades
Players fit for action
Referee ready to blow his whistle
No ice!

Dafydd Press (11)
Gors Junior School

SNOWMAN

Stripy blue hat
Checked scarf
Fresh carrot
Seven black raisins
Three lumps of coal
Two long sticks
No snow!

Sarah Kervin (11)
Gors Junior School

TIREDNESS

My tiredness is as white as a soft quilt
It tastes like a sweet sugar lump
It smells like some wine just from the bottle
My tiredness looks like a swirly wave on the sea
And sounds like a whistle whistling sweet tunes
It feels like when you put your hand into twisty water.

Matthew Thomas (10)
Gors Junior School

BINGO

Marking off numbers
Full house, line
People waiting anxiously
No win!

Christopher Hookway (11)
Gors Junior School

WHAT IS THE MOON?

A little red cherry sitting on a branch.
A giant golden egg dripping on black toast.
A bright yellow banana hanging on a dark tree.
A silver golf ball laying on a muddy golf course
A round yellow dartboard standing on a black wall
A juicy yellow lemon laying on a blue bowl
A round fat wheel whizzing on a flat road
A salty cheese pizza waiting to be eaten.

Kylie Evans (10)
Mayhill Junior School

THE SUN

Scientists say that the sun is a body
of condensed hydrogen gas with a
diameter of 864,000 miles and a
surface temperature of 6,000 degrees
centigrade. These are the facts I know
but I also know that when I see his
yellow light it is making all the
world happy and bright. It is the
making of creation.

Lindsey Lerwell (9)
Mayhill Junior School

PLANETS

Venus is so white,
Saturn has a ring round it
Pluto is so small like me.

Daniel Evans (8)
Mayhill Junior School

THE MOON

Ball of dust in space
It's thousands of miles away
Beautiful white moon.

Christopher Davies (8)
Mayhill Junior School

SATURN

Large planet Saturn
With an icy ring round it
It's made out of gas.

Christopher Courtney (8)
Mayhill Junior School

MOON

The moon is shining
a beautiful ball of rock
glistening in space.

Gemma Underhill (8)
Mayhill Junior School

REFLECTIONS

Reflections at night
So colourful and so bright
A beautiful gleam.

Jenna Grove (8)
Mayhill Junior School

STARS

Sparkling all the time.
Stars sparkling in the dark night.
The stars give us light.

Kimberley Martin (8)
Mayhill Junior School

STARS

Beautiful and bright
It is shining down on me
Light for us to see.

Jodie Ford (8)
Mayhill Junior School

ASTRAL FLOWERS

Far away in a land nearer to heaven than to
                                  Earth on a planet named Jupiter,
Astral flowers grow,
Voluminous and luminous draping dappled
                                  buds which hang from corkscrew stems,
A mass of entwined colours tease your eyes as
                                  you stare at the star shaped plants,

Lamp lit tendril stamens light the strange unknown Earth,
Decorated with crystal coloured dew
Gracefully they sway in the shadowy beams of the moon.

A slight breeze comes from a windmill shaped plant
Slowly the multicoloured petals fall to the ground,
Allowing themselves to be covered by the fluorescent snow,

The world I know so well shall sleep
Forgotten till the spring,
The colours go,
Stems fall low,
Sleep strange garden sleep
Till time retreats

Tennille Rees (10)
Oakleigh House School

THE WINNER

I sit calmly waiting
Quick breathing,
Knees shaking,
Heart pounding.
Oh, no I am next!
I have it all
My music, an audience and my piano.
I wish I could go home!
Now it's my turn.
I stand up shakily,
Walk to the piano and put down the music.
My fingers hang poised
Above the smooth, shiny black and white keys.
I take a deep breath and start to play.
The piano starts to sing.
A lovely melody, I start to dream.
The notes are beautiful.
The end has come, I could have played forever!
The judges are in a huddle
Nail-biting tension; who will win?
Suddenly it's announced
Triumph is within my grasp
For I'm the winner, yes, it's me!

Jane Vancura (10)
Oakleigh House School

ASTRAL FLOWERS

A contrast of colour from the bud,
Like tentacles, climbing out swaying stretching for the moon,
Fluorescent coloured petals expanding in space,
A star shaped flower appears,
With a meandering stem of emerald green,

A shower of dewdrops sparkling in the moonlight falls to the floor,
Another flower appears pendulous,
Gleaming, shining with falling petals
Dappled, spotted, mottled flowers,
Their stems elongated climbing ever upwards.

Myriad colours glow in the moonlight,
Voluminous leaves clutch nearby stems,
Luscious flowers sway to the music of the sphere,
Making a timeless melody.

Lucy Bassett (10)
Oakleigh House School

ASTRAL FLOWERS

High up in the astral world
The flowers dance and swirl
Showing of their rainbow petals.
Webs of dew cover the ground.
Tinkling bells, fireworks of colour.
The astral carnival has begun.
Tendrils trumpet,
And red, orange and yellow clowns
Spread their fragrant petals
White and pink dancers pirouette.
A scarlet flower opens his case of green foliage
And emerges into the light.
Silver vines look like tentacles.

While caterpillar stems crawl over rocks
From Earth, space looks dark and bleak
But if you could only see the colours and
Plants of the astral world
You too would be amazed
By their great beauty.

Sophie Batty (11)
Oakleigh House School

WRITING A POEM

I'm trying to write a poem on a sunny Saturday afternoon.
I'm hating waiting for ideas to come.
I bet that Dylan Thomas didn't have
Problems like these sitting under Cwmdonkin's trees.
I wish he was in Green house
Then he could write the poem for me.

It's getting very dark now. I can almost see the moon.
I'm getting rather sleepy in this comfy warm room.
My mum's completely useless, she's really gone to pot.
I'm getting quite frustrated and it's really rather hot.

Writing this poem on a dark Saturday evening.
Yes I'm still writing that poem.
It's getting on my nerves
I think I need some help now . . .
Dad!

Flora McKay (8)
Oakleigh House School

ASTRAL FLOWERS

Glowing blossoms in a haze,

Voluminous tendrils of sapphire blue.
Hanging, gleaming elegantly,
Myriad coloured crystal dew.
Luminescent pollen topples down,
And emerging still . . .
Is a carnival of flowers, gaudy colours,
Dappled and mottled.
Some like shells of amber, ruby, copper, gold.
Some in images of blown bubbles.
Floating up and up, heavenwards!
To anyone else it is translucently obvious,
Swinging and swaying in a way.
Which we recognise.
Many petalled, different shapes.
Nectar so sweet smelling,
So tempting and inviting.

Glowing blossoms in a haze.

Amy Ward (11)
Oakleigh House School

ASTRAL FLOWERS

A profusion of colours,
Each one mottled with a fingertip of magenta,
Moonlight bringing out tendrils of colour,
Stems meandering reaching out in the moonlight,
Shades of myriad colours mingle,
Each petal with a moonlight lining,
Sugar crystals sifted over these astral beings,
Masses of colour blending into another,
Elegant flowers vertical and erect,
Each petal dripping with beauty in the everlasting moonlight,
Astral flowers in a moonlit astral landscape.

Holly Nicholas (11)
Oakleigh House School

ASTRAL FLOWERS

It is morning in this astral world
The glowing corkscrew stems swaying in eternity
The blossoms dangle from fingers of a stretching out branch
The dappled tendrils shake like tentacles
While masses of green, purple and blue petals expand
The lavender flowers are dripping with the cold fresh crystal dew
The gaudy flower heads, tight, blanketed buds with
                    their magnificent stamens, now rebelled
Today there is a haze in the air,
A misty whiteness hanging in suspension above,
The astral planet spinning in space.

Julia Heath-Davies (11)
Oakleigh House School

ASTRAL FLOWERS

Masses of foliage forming
A profusion of colour.
Blossoms sparkling with crystal beads.
Dappled petals dripping with dew,
Brightly coloured flowers,
Making a carnival of colours,
In the glade of blossoms.
Glowing stems wind upwards,
Entwining tendrils into a luxuriant mass.
Delicate petals hang downwards,
Silhouetted against the moonlight.
Luminescent fronds dance
In the deep sapphire sky.
Gaudy flowers with tooth-edged leaves,
All shades of moonlight colours,
Each plaited shape interweaving,
Forming deep pools of shadows.
Light and dark contrasting in time and space.

Rosanna Zorko (10)
Oakleigh House School

SPRING, THE CONQUEROR

Winter sits on his icy throne
Everything about him touched with cold
No shoot, no bud, no flower blooms.
Each single droplet turned to ice.
Earth like metal, hard and cold.
Then spring fights back,
A multitude of warm rays
Breaking through, melting winter's hold,
Touching each plant, making it grow
And sprout its shoot through the wintry ground.
First the timid snowdrop,
Trembling in winter's chilly breath,
Soon followed by bold crocuses,
Vivid purple and brilliant gold,
Opening their oval petals,
Showing their bright colours and great splendour,
Overhead catkins are suspended
From their long spindly stems
Like dangling banners.
All spring's troops are gathered
And as the days get longer
Spring marches victorious in the sunshine
Defying the cruel reign of winter.

Louise Rowley (11)
Oakleigh House School

ASTRAL FLOWERS

A tiny seed hidden deep in the ground
Drops of water woke from its deep sleep
The casing breaks open and now
The plant starts to emerge
First long green stems
Stretching for the moonlight
Their glowing colours
Gleaming in the moonlight
Their petals are shaped
Like little aliens
Their colours vivid and vibrant
A multicolour of sapphire,
Crimson, azure and bronze
They sway from their
Corkscrew stems
Twining up and down
Towards the plant.

Alex Roberts (11)
Oakleigh House School

THE WINNER

The last two laps,
Only one more,
I had to do it,
Speed was all I needed,
(Shoving), bumping, jostling, pushing,
My pulse beating every second.
I could see the others only seconds behind,
I turned the bend, my body burning,
In front of me was a blur of colours,
This was it, would I be this year's winner?
I felt a spirit pushing me on,
My legs tired but I kept on running,
I aimed at the tape,
Snapped through the ribbon,
I had done it, hooray!
I fell down and cried with excitement,
A cheer went up,
Hands were clapping,
I had won!
I felt on top of the world!

Jacqueline Bassett (10)
Oakleigh House School

THE WINNER

The wonderful exciting moment has arrived
The sun was dazzling orange
And brilliant blinding yellow
A wonderful day for a new beginning.
He was lying there, damp and trembling.
His sweet mother nuzzled him
With her soft muzzle,
Whinnying gently,
Pushing him forward.
His long straggly legs
Have no strength at all.
He rises, wobbly, trembling with excitement
He, limping, takes a brand new step
Into the sunlight,
Every minute something new.
Some skill to learn.
Some fresh goal to reach.
Just for today he's brand new,
But tomorrow, just wait and see.
Here we have a winner!

Stephanie Wookey (10)
Oakleigh House School

MAM

My mam Doris
Has eyes like jewels, sparkling and bright,
Kind gentle and soothing.
Her skin is like silk
When she kisses me
It's soft to touch,
Though she has wrinkles in parts.
My mam Doris
Always smiles,
Never frowns.
She's a wise old teddy
That you would love to hug.
She loves me, cherishes me.
Never makes me feel down.
I go to see her when I'm sad,
She cheers me up with tales of long ago.
My special mam Doris
Has kind ways, thinking of herself last.
She thinks of me as her little drop of sunlight
She has a name for me
'Sugar plum fairy'
She does unusual things
She uses her teabag twice
And treasures all my school work,
She stores a tin full of chocolate in the fridge
(Especially for me)
My mam Doris
What makes her different from other grans?
What makes a robin different from a sparrow?

I love my mam Doris

Emilie Williams (11)
Pengelli Primary School

SHINY

Shiny are the fresh chestnuts
On a breezy autumn day.
Shiny is the glistening sequins
On a glamorous dress
Moving in rhythm, twinkling on the
Dance floor.
Shiny is the bright, glossy tinsel
Hanging on an emerald green fir tree
Topped with a twinkling star at
Christmas time.
Shiny is the gentle dew
On a cold bitter morning.

But, the shiniest of all,
Is the twinkle in my
Baby niece's crystal-blue eyes,
Glistening whenever she smiles.

Stephanie Thomson (11)
Pengelli Primary School

MOON FLIGHT

I feel very brave
But sad, dejected
And so isolated
Alone,
I'm the one circling the moon.
No one will remember me
I am lost in the depths of
Space.

Stuart Mindt (10)
Pengelli Primary School

WHAT IS A STAR?

What is a star?
Hot burning gas?
Or is it
A sprinkle of glitter?
Who knows?
What is a star?
A ball of fire?
Or is it
God switching the lights
On and off?
Who knows?

Owen James (9)
Pengelli Primary School

ALIENS

Do you think strange creatures live on Mars
Or on hot planets that orbit the stars?
Is there a place where monsters are green
Or pink spotted aliens can be seen?
Maybe one day they'll come down from space
And pay a visit to the human race.
What will they think of what they see?
What will they think of you and me?

Scott Thomas (10)
Pengelli Primary School

RAIN

Hear that rain pattering on the house.
Nothing to do except draw.
Draw funny flowers on the steamy windows.
Lights are on in the middle of the day.
Gloomy colours everywhere,
Darkness in the house
Old people have pains, they say.
No netball matches to play
No riding bikes all day.
I hate the rain.

But,
See it glittering on the leaves,
Shining like jewels on the grass,
Watering the crops, feeding lakes,
Listen to the rhythms on the roofs.
I love the rain.

Christina Evans (10)
Pengelli Primary School

THE CHRISTMAS TABLE

A red silk cloth
on the table,
crisps and popcorn and jelly,
big platefuls of jelly
and a great big chicken.
Ice-cream,
lots of ice-cream
with bananas and cream
lots of cream.

Mark Owens (10)
Pengelli Primary School

WIND AND RAIN

It's cold outside
It's raining
The rain is swooshing down the gutters
Every drop as cold as me.
It's cold outside
The rain feeds the river
That flows into the sea.
It's cold outside
I run my finger down the condensation
As I watch the rain fall.
It's cold outside
But it helps flowers and crops.
It's cold outside
And raining
The netball's called off
It's warm out now
The birds are singing
I can go out now and play again.

Annie Lee
Pengelli Primary School

FEAR

Fear is a snarling beast hiding behind the bike sheds, hideous
in the morning light.
Fear is a roaring fire burning *all* sense of security.
Fear is a tidal wave wiping out *all* grains of bravery.
Fear is a lashing rain washing away *all* hope.
Fear is a volcano melting *all* feeling of happiness.
Fear is a thundering wind tearing your world apart.

Sam Batsford (11)
Pengelli Primary School

THE BULLY AND THE VICTIM

'He's beating me.'
'I do it
Because I'm king of the playground.'
'He's left me out of games.'
'I do it
Because all my friends think I'm hard.'
'I dare not go out
In case he pounces on me.'
'I love using violence.
Tormenting and intimidating.'
'I feel insecure.
I feel left out.'
'I do it
When he feels insecure.'
'I am too frightened to go to the toilet in school
Because he might threaten me.'
'I do it
When he is lonely in the playground.
I feel great.
I feel on top of the world.'
'I go home crying every day.
I feel like attacking someone soon.
Annoying people and beating.'
'I'm in shock in all situations.'
'I feel like upsetting him
Intimidating my victim'
'I'm being bullied.'

Christopher Hinchey (11)
Pengelli Primary School

SPACE FLIGHT

I'd like to be an astronaut
To see the shiny stars,
I'd zoom around the galaxy
And even visit Mars.
I'd surely meet some aliens
My friends they'd get to be.
I wonder if my mummy
Would let them home for tea.

Kenneth Rees (10)
Pengelli Primary School

THE WIND

Endless days of calm,
Not a leaf trembles,
Not a flower bending its narrow head.

Then the wind came.
The leaves started to bluster
Became trapped in corners by the walls.
The flowers' petals blew off into the darkness.

The wind worsened.
Destroying the animals' homes.
Destroying their security
The candyfloss cloud was no more,
It burst
Dropping inky black rain.

James Evans (11)
Pengelli Primary School

THE ALIEN

Slimy gunge pours out as
Three eyes stare at you
High cheek bones on his lumpy face
Ten arms swirl all over the place
Fire bursts out of his pointed ears.

Jenna Pugh (10)
Pengelli Primary School

WHAT IS A STAR?

What is a star?
A wild nuclear reaction?
Or is it
God's gift to voyagers, guiding them on their quests?
What is a star?
A cloud of bubbling acid?
Or is it
A raging firework burning with scarlet and crimson flames?
What is a star?
A burst of poisonous gases?
Or is it
The eyes of a predator stalking the planet Earth?
What is a star?
A cluster of violent atoms?
Or is it
A street light on the road to God's palace?

David Morris (11)
Pengelli Primary School

RAIN

Lots of little raindrops
Sparkling on the spider's web
Jewel-like it glistens
Sparkling in the garden
Lots of little raindrops
Racing down the gutter
And on my bedroom window
Lots of little raindrops
Dancing to the rhythm.

Scott Roberts
Pengelli Primary School

WHAT IS A DAFFODIL?

A golden yellow flower
Trumpet shaped
Inside its long green stem
Slimy, wet dribbly sap climbs
Climbs to the seed box at the top
It floats in the wind
'Come inside my trumpet,'
It says to the bees.

Cheryl Davies (11)
Pengelli Primary School

TIME TRAVELLER

Round and round the spiralling stones,
Back two thousand two hundred years.
I see
The circular huts with the smoke
Drifting through the top,
Men practising with blue spiral patterns,
On their faces.
Golden shields for defence
And still I stand there watching
I hear
Ladies chatting as they weave,
Men practising for war,
Shouting as they practise,
Children arguing.
And still I stand there listening
I smell
Hot cawl sizzling in the pot,
Smoke from the fire,
And still I stand there waiting.
I feel
Welcome and at home.
And then my journey ends.
I leave the Celtic village
Returning to the present.

Michelle Planck (10)
Pengelli Primary School

WHAT IS A STAR?

What is a star?
A great ball of lightning flashing in the darkness.
Or is it.
A huge mass of honey sticking to a great black hive?
What is a star?
A hot ball of burning fire?
Or is it
Sequins glued to a black sheet?
What is a star?
A ball of gas floating in the atmosphere?
Or is it
A pack of fireworks exploding in God's display?
What is a star?
A light-year of meteors?
Or is it.
A jewel sparkling from a Goddess's dress?
What is a star?
A circle of yellow gas ringed in air?
Or is it.
Sprinkles of glitter skating over paper?
What is a star?
A heat rash of light?
Or is it.
God's guide's torch-light showing the way to heaven?
Who knows?

Lewis Evans (10)
Pengelli Primary School

REFLECTION

When I look in the mirror
There is someone there
I don't know who.
She looks like me
But . . .
When I put my left hand up
The person in the mirror
Puts up her right hand.

Charlotte Thomas (10)
Pengelli Primary School

THE SEA HAS MANY MOODS

Lapping gently wave over wave
Flowing across gently swaying like it was singing a song
Drifting as if it was in a world of its own
Whispering 'Can you hear me?'
Crying as if he had been beaten
Dashing fiercely against the great tall and wide cliff
Crunching the sand on the floor
It swishes the shells around and around
It is like it is kissing the little boats
It is as if it hugs the fish when it is cold.

Jason Garrett (11)
St Joseph's Cathedral School

THE SEA

I am the master
who controls the sea,
I'm as old as the universe and
every landscape on Earth,
I come from the rivers, lakes and ponds,
my family are the rocks and seaweed.
My friends are the fishes, whales,
sharks and octopuses and all other kinds of animals.
Worst of all are the enemies, the ones who pollute me
and spill oil in me.
I eat sand and stones and sometimes dead fish of the sea.
I like the gazing sun that shines down on me,
I hate the thunderstorms which throw me about.
I am calm on a warm summer's night when
the fish are asleep and everything's still.
I am angry when the rain is beating heavily
and bits of snow are falling on me.

Laura Davies (10)
St Joseph's Cathedral School

PERFECT PIZZA

Pizza is perfect in all sorts of ways,
It makes you wish, you could eat it for days and days.
It's hot and delicious, tasty and good,
You should try it, you really should.
It smells like paradise and tastes like it too,
That's why you should try it, it's gorgeous food.

Lauren Thomas (10)
St Joseph's Cathedral School

MIGHTY POWERFUL PACIFIC

I am the mighty powerful Pacific, seaweed and coral creator,
I am as old as the Earth, from when it was born,
Before dinosaurs and plants, creators big or small, anywhere,
I come from our mighty God, the mighty father of all the universe,
I was born as the smallest river, I have been up in the sky as rain,
I have got a family of seaweed, rocks, fish, and much wildlife,
I get my energy from the sun and stars, and I look to
my mother and father,
sun and moon,
My friends are the small rivers, and dolphins and whales,
But my enemies I hate, they're man, litter, rubbish,
oil and waste they do not want.
I have a diet of dead creatures which I turn into sand,
I eat what is in me.
I enjoy sweeping the sand in and out, crushing rocks,
and seeing new life, I also enjoy making caves,
I hate being polluted, or being told what to do.
At the calmest time, when on a night full of stars,
I glisten through the sea water.
When the sea horses tickle me, and swim through the layers,
So light I cannot feel them, but when it is stormy,
I become afraid, I gather my family and friends,
The heavy rain hurts my soft skin, it makes me angry,
On the calmest of days I do not have time to sleep,
I push water back and forth, boats in and out,
At the end of a day, I close my eyes delicately for a second
and wonder far into the night,
I wonder hard at what would happen next.

Angharad Fowler (10)
St Joseph's Cathedral School

SPACE

All alone in a neverending black void
As dark as night
No living being
Just meteorites hurtling
Through my black wilderness.

A flicker of light
From a rocket far away
Just floating around in space
All alone in a secret wilderness.

James Morgan (11)
St Joseph's Cathedral School

LORD PACIFIC

I am the Lord Pacific, animal protector, sand cleaner.
Older than you, old as rock,
From the small sea horse to the mighty whale,
They are my family.
Sparkly ponds and lakes flow by me make me flow far,
Oil, glass, rubbish are my big enemies,
I like kids playing at my mouth.
I bring in rocks to grind and munch,
But I hate man poisons
I am calm on warm days because people play,
But when it is cold it is hard to sleep and it is rough.

Sean Voyle (10)
St Joseph's Cathedral School

MY FOX

His body slithers through the long green grass,
Like an unknown shadow,
Stretching his long strong legs and leaping into
The air like a feather,
Gliding onto his prey and killing swiftly and quickly.
That's my fox.

Crawling through the bushes,
Silently targeting its prey
With vicious teeth, sword-sharp
Plunging at the poor helpless animal.
Killing it in seconds
That's my fox.

Hidden in a blanket of darkness
Protecting his youth
He is free as the wind
A shadow in the darkness
With his ghostly coat
That's my fox.

Paul King (10)
St Joseph's Cathedral School

MOODS OF THE SEA

Bashing fiercely against the sharp rocks,
Pulling the tide madly back and forth,
Splashing hard on the smooth sea,
Wearing the coastline,
Crunching the rocks in anger,
Crashing the sea against the sand.

Lapping gently over and over,
Whispering softly 'Come in, come in,'
Washing the dirt and the rubbish away,
Swaying side to side,
Flowing under the moonlight.

Jodie Boyes (11)
St Joseph's Cathedral School

I AM . . .

I am a school
A tall cream building on top of a hill
With a yard where children play
Guarding the school is the figure of the
Headmaster

I am the headmaster short and fat
In charge of all the teachers

We are the teachers who teach the children

We are the children learning our work
Going to church

I am the church a majestic cathedral
With nuns and priests
Where people come to worship God

I am the God
Creator of every Holy person.

Kirsty Evans (10)
St Joseph's Cathedral School

ABOUT THE OCEAN

I am the ocean,
I am surrounded with a rolling and crashing
blue and green sea full of brightly coloured fish,
edged with a golden sand
and happy people.

I am the people,
playing joyfully on the soft silky sand
splashing around in the deep blue sea
whilst sun bathing on the smooth golden sand
with the sun beating down on me.

I am the boiling hot burning sun,
I am the bright orange fiery sun
glistening in the bright blue sky,
sometimes white fluffy clouds creep over me,
then I cannot be seen
the sky looks dull without me
but when I'm out shining bright
I beat down on the blue greeny ocean.

I am the blue greeny ocean
I am usually very calm and gentle,
I very gently go in and out of cracks in caves
taking rubbish to and fro.

Shells, pearls, golden treasure chests and fish
live deep within me.

I am the colourful fish
I weave in and out of seaweed,
Quickly and quietly
Exploring unknown caves
Deep down in the ocean
In our mysterious world.

Siobhan Williams (11)
St Joseph's Cathedral School

I Am The . . .

I am the trumpeter playing as hard as I can,
I am the trumpet showing off my shine in the band,
I am the band:
I am the band playing rock and roll,
I am the rock and roll:
I am the rock and roll thinking I'm better than the
classical tune,
I am the classical tune crying my heart out trying
to win a concert,
I am the concert,
I am the concert with pop music, jazz and classics too,
Take your pick it's up to you.

Jason Trueman (11)
St Joseph's Cathedral School

Alone In The Moonlight

Alone in the moonlight
The moon sparkling like a round crystal
It swiftly moves through the sky like a yacht
The moonlit garden lights up the house
And shines like the sun setting
The shadows creep up and deform shapes
Twigs snapping like crocodiles' teeth
Wolves howling on the cliffs
The feeling is frightening
Like being locked up in jail.

Gabrielle Browne (9)
St Joseph's Cathedral School

THE SEA FATHER

I am the mighty father of all oceans and all creatures in it,
I am as old as time itself when the first movement was made,
I come from the stars they shine on me and give me strength.
My mother sun and father moon and all rivers and ponds are family.
My friends the sand, seaweed and fish guide me through
This endless life.

My enemies are man and their pollution,
I swallow them as they drown and die,
I eat rocks off the defenceless cliff face.
I like playing with my friends,
I kiss the sand and drink from rock pools.
I hate it when it is too hot,
I love it when it's cool and calm.
When I am calm I stroll on the beach,
When I am angry I love to destroy every cliff in
Sight!

Norena McCready (11)
St Joseph's Cathedral School

THE SEA HAS MANY MOODS

The sea has many moods:
Smashing wildly against the rocks,
Dashing against the high sea wall,
Lashing at the fishing boats
Wilder than anything,
Crushing the jagged rocks under the sea
Swaying side to side,
Lapping over and over again.

Ben Davies (10)
St Joseph's Cathedral School

PERSONIFYING THE SEA

I am the soft and gentle Pacific Ocean
I flow like a pond, and splash like a child
Old as the sun, born before human
I have the fish, the sand as my friends
Pollution is my enemy
I eat sunken boats
I am very angry when people leave
my beach a mess
Calm when my friends came from
house to house to swim and have fun
My family is the soft sand and smooth rocks
My aunt and uncle live in the Atlantic and Indian Oceans
I hate people who fish for fish because
they are my friends
I like my friends and I play in the sea
I come from Swansea bay.

Nicola Marsh (10)
St Joseph's Cathedral School

THINGS ABOUT SPACE

In the black misty smoke a moon fades,
He is like a hundred year old balloon,
A rocket zooms and blooms,
A constellation is like a spider's trick,
Empty in that keyhole a flash comes and goes.

Jon-Paul Wayne-Morris (10)
St Joseph's Cathedral School

THE SEA HAS MANY MOODS

The sea has many moods,
Crashing dangerously against the crumbling walls,
Bashing fiercely against all of the innocent houses,
Smashing every glistening window,
Crushing all the rocks one after another,
Splashing all the surfy people off their surfboards,
Frothing the sea bed, all shining white.

Peaceful,
Lapping calmly over the sand,
Flowing gently across the beautiful fish,
Drifting onto all the crumbly rocks,
Swaying side to side,
Whispering to all the people strolling along the beach,
Carrying all kinds of interesting things.

Charlotte Evans (11)
St Joseph's Cathedral School

MOODS OF THE SEA

The sea has many moods,
Dashing wildly to the crooked rocks,
Bashing the boats to pieces like a tiger attacking a human,
Rushing eagerly to the golden sand waiting for the signal,
Smashing beautiful homes to ribbons,
Crashing into wonderful strong men who want to
fight this really terrible storm.

The sea has many moods,
Crying to witness the cry of the seagulls,
Flowing at the bottom of the golden sun,
Drifting on the surface waiting for someone to sail,
Carrying disgusting waste and garbage,
With a sparkle of sunlight,
Whispering a sound that carefully flows into your ears.

Sarah Lloyd (10)
St Joseph's Cathedral School

THE SEA

I am the one who carves the rocks to make them round,
Older than you can imagine,
I come from only myself,
Related to all the great oceans and seas,
My friends are the fish who swim inside my stomach,
The starfish who live in my head,
The sharks, whales and dolphins,
Who play happily jumping inside my head,
The sharks are the most endangered species,
But the creature *I hate* is the human being,
I drown them if they come near me,
Some are saved by other humans,
I eat the seaweed that I wash in,
I am calm when humans don't pollute me,
I am angry when people try to stamp on me,
I hold my breath but then I blow,
I grab them,
Then I set the current onto them,
This is the time I am happy.

Charlotte Rogers (10)
St Joseph's Cathedral School

THE COLD ANTARCTIC

I am the cold Antarctic, ice melter, sand sweeper,
Warrior of water.
Old as the earth, before life and man.
My family are other oceans around the world,
My friends are lakes, rivers and waterfalls.
I have enemies, like men and their tankers,
I make a big storm and throw them about.
I eat the icebergs and ships,
The turtles, sharks, fish and lobsters
Swimming around my stomach,
I do not mind at all.
I hate the ships that men create,
It gets on my nerves.

Daniel Lacey (11)
St Joseph's Cathedral School

MOODS OF THE SEA

The sea has many moods,
Flowing slowly as the sun shines brightly,
Swaying back and fore, the dolphins come to say hello,
Lapping wave after wave,
Drifting as the crabs swim underneath,
Whispering my name again and again,
Crying because people pollute her.

Crunching the big heavy rocks ferociously,
Bashing against the coastline,
Rushing as the wind blows its hardest,
Munching the golden sand,
Smashing down the big grey cliffs,
Crashing harshly against big colourful boats.

Alix Scrine (10)
St Joseph's Cathedral School

MY MUM'S THUMB

My mum's thumb
can bend right back
it can crush a grape
in one stroke
and break up sticks without
getting a splinter.

If it wanted
it could be a potato peeler
or a baby dummy
a butter spreader or a fruit juice squeezer.

It's already a great digit
and if it dressed up
it could easily pass as a plum or a cherry.

In actual fact it's quite simply
the world's best waver.

James Matthews (10)
St Joseph's Cathedral School

THE MIGHTY PACIFIC

I am the mighty Pacific Ocean.
I fear nothing but pollution.
Animals have nothing to fear.
I am as old and as prehistoric as the dinosaurs.
I come from my deep blue sea.
With huge crashing waves, I splutter about.
My family are the Atlantic, Indian and Arctic Oceans.
They roam through all the world.
My friends are creatures in the water
That sparkle and swim.
I have enemies called humans,
Who pollute my waters with oil.
No care they have for the deep Pacific sea.
I crunch on rocks and chew on ships.
I like clean waters to be proud of.
Then I will be calm forever.

Adam Davies-Cross (10)
St Joseph's Cathedral School

IF I COULD

If I could hear a cry for help from the tallest peak,
I could hear what's happening for the rest of the week.
If I could hear people talk,
I could hear the little ants walk.
If I could hear all these things
I could hear a bird flapping its wings.

If I could see for miles and miles
I could see everyone's smiles.
If I could see the moles playing around
I could see underground
If I could see all these things,
Wouldn't life be great.

Carys Evans (10)
St Joseph's Cathedral School

I'LL TELL YOU WHAT FRIGHTENS ME

I'll tell you what frightens me,
Shadows in my room at night frighten me,
The ghastly sound of wind creeping through the window,
That's what frightens me.

I'll tell you what frightens me,
Walking down a dark alleyway,
With nobody seen in sight,
Suddenly the light comes on and my shadow gives me a fright.

I'm walking through the graveyard,
With ghouls all around,
Aggh! There's a hand coming from the ground
There's ghosts all around me,
And monsters everywhere,
Oh look over there,
I'm sure that's Mrs Saer.

Thomas White (10)
St Joseph's Cathedral School

A THREE COURSE MEAL

Yum, yum, yum, what's for dinner?
Mmmmm pasta for me it's a winner.
The lovely sauce to go on top,
Red, spicy sauce, I like it a lot.

The cooked dinner is up next,
The word stunning in big, bold text.
The round crispy potatoes drowned in gravy,
The golden Yorkshires, shall I start with? Maybe.
The gorgeous green veg, certainly,
The scrumptious smell, I'm still hungry.

The chocolate cake should fill me up,
Better than hot chocolate in a cup.
The round, brown cake, just the right size,
It smells so sweet, aren't I wise.

My dinner was so delicious,
If I said it wasn't, Mum would turn vicious.

Michael Jones (10)
St Joseph's Cathedral School

LIGHTNING

Lightning, lightning I'm scared of lightning,
It is very frightening,
It comes with thunder,
It makes me wonder why it comes,
It sounds very much like drums.

Lightning, lightning I'm scared of lightning,
It is very frightening,
It is very, very loud,
It makes me quite proud,
To live in Wales,
With all the lightning tales.

Katie Burton (9)
St Joseph's Cathedral School

THUNDER AND LIGHTNING

In the middle of the night,
When rain is pattering down,
A loud flash and rumble,
Storms are coming to town.

The lightning lights up the room,
Cackle crack cackle boom,
Thunder comes what a bang!
As loud as an earthquake,
What a clang!

Lying alone, listening carefully,
As the thunder and lightning frightens me,
Its flash, its bang, the heavy rain,
I never want to be in a storm again.

Laura Martin (10)
St Joseph's Cathedral School

I'LL TELL YOU WHAT FRIGHTENS ME

I'll tell you what frightens me,
A vampire sucking the blood of Penelope.
A werewolf with those hellish jaws,
A six foot monster with giant claws.
A scary wood which seems to come alive,
A mad-man with a pointy knife.
A horrible monster with just one eye,
The Devil who makes people fry.
Cannibals stirring away at something hot,
Oh no! I think it's Scott!

Dean Harris (9)
St Joseph's Cathedral School

IF I COULD . . .

If I could hear someone talk,
I could hear someone walk.
If I could hear someone sneeze,
I could hear the slightest breeze.

If I could touch a burning fire,
I could tell who is a liar.
If I could touch some sticky glue,
I could touch the sea so blue.

If I could see what's in the past,
I could see who was last.

Maybelle Morris (10)
St Joseph's Cathedral School

I'LL TELL YOU WHAT FRIGHTENS ME!

I'll tell you what frightens me,
Shadows on the wall at night frighten me,
And owls that fly, the wind that howls,
And even the milkman frightens me.

I'll tell you what frightens me,
The tramps on the street frighten me,
And insects that crawl, and shapes on the wall
And even a policeman frightens me.

I'll tell you what frightens me,
The snakes in the grass frighten me,
The smell of burning rubber, and people who hate
each other,
And even heights frighten me.

Christina Charalambou (10)
St Joseph's Cathedral School

FEAR

The colour is black,
It tastes like hot toast burnt,
It smells like books that have been in rubbish bins,
It sounds like rustling trees,
It feels like someone following behind me.

Saira Souliman (9)
St Joseph's Cathedral School

THUNDER AND LIGHTNING

It's time for thunder and lightning,
So thunder hits lightning,
Children scream,
Grannies faint,
Down in the kitchen crack goes a plate.

1, 2, 3 down goes a tree,
Mum! Quick the roof's got hit.
Dad calls for me,
I run quick,
But all of a sudden the thunder and lightning,
Makes a big bang!
Sadly it hit my neighbour's van.

Thunder and lightning,
When will it end?
It keeps making noises over again.

Elizabeth Collins (10)
St Joseph's Cathedral School

SNOWING

It is snowing outside,
The temperature is minus five.
It's bright and white,
People have snow fights,
When it's snowing in the morning.

It is cold and peaceful,
Silent and relaxing,
Like a path of glass,
Made by little snowflakes,
When it's snowing in the morning.

Laura Frost (9)
St Joseph's Cathedral School

FRAGMENTED POEM

I am the world,
I hold all the oceans
and all the continents.

I am the continents,
I am filled with cities and towns,
and overflowing with people.

I am a person,
I walk around everyday,
I share a world with insects.

I am an insect,
crawling about buildings and countryside,
with my shell protecting me from other insects,
I don't like dust covering me.

I am dust,
covering worktops and cupboards,
I die when someone blows or wipes me.

Daniel Penman (11)
St Joseph's Cathedral School

WHAT COULD WE SEE

We could see lots of tempting things
Pretty flowers, children on swinging swings
Long winter days
Cold and damp
Rain pouring deep down
Flooding street lamps

We could see
Leaves flying by
Street lights flashing
High in the strong sky

We could see
Leaves changing colour in the trees
The windscreens on cars all frantically freeze
People rushing from here to there
To get out of the cold crisp Arctic air.

Laura Martin (9)
St Joseph's Cathedral School

THUNDER AND LIGHTNING

Thunder and lightning lights up my room,
With a crash and a bang all at once.
Rolling, tumbling, scares me to death.
Blue flashes everywhere I look.

The lights go on and off,
I roll back and forth,
There was a slam coming from the porch,
It's only Mum.

Scott Hart (10)
St Joseph's Cathedral School

DELICIOUS CREAMY RICE

Delicious creamy rice,
In a rich golden cream,
With chicken on the side,
Oh what a dream.
The smell of it is fabulous,
Impossible to describe,
It looks like little treasures,
You find in the sand.
Its taste's so scrumptious,
I'd have it every night,
It smells like chicken,
That has just been fried.
It is so lovely I'd eat it everywhere I go,
In restaurants and cafes,
And even down my Uncle Joe's.

Emma Carlsen (10)
St Joseph's Cathedral School

THUNDER AND LIGHTNING

Lights flicker with a rumble,
Then comes a bang!
Strong winds are coming,
Oh no the window's cracked!

Loads of water coming through,
Quick get the covers.
In my bed I'm thinking,
Thinking what happens next.

James Meade (9)
St Joseph's Cathedral School

CHICKENPOX

I hate having chickenpox
It really makes me itch.
I hate having spots on me
It really makes me twitch.

I hate them on my legs
Popping out on my hands
I hate them on my face
Frightening all my fans.

Emma Thomas (10)
St Joseph's Cathedral School

PACIFIC OCEAN

My name is the Pacific Ocean
I was born in a block of ice
I am millions of years old
The dolphin is my sister and the shark is my brother
The river and the rain are in my family
I can go everywhere
I do not get smaller I get bigger because of the rain
The ships and the submarines give me pains
The fish and the octopus makes me happy
The weather makes me calm
I don't eat
I don't sleep
People like me when I am calm.

Martin Goold (10)
St Joseph's Cathedral School

I Am The Sea

I am the sea
Blue and green,
I came in on the beach.

I am the beach
Creamy sand,
Some pink some white,
Some blue sea shells.

I am the sea shells,
Inside me is a small crab.

I am the crab,
I run to the pools,
And I land in the sea.

Sarah Martin (10)
St Joseph's Cathedral School

I'll Tell You What Frightens Me . . .

I'll tell you what frightens me, thunder,
Thunder sounds like the Earth is going to end.
I'll tell you what frightens me, vertigo,
Vertigo makes me so sick.
I'll tell you what frightens me, spiders,
Spiders that are hairy and crawl all over me.
I'll tell you what frightens me, wars,
Wars when people get killed by bombs,
Softly dropping all around, that's what frightens me.

Nicholas Taylor (9)
St Joseph's Cathedral School

ME

How tall am I?
My mum says I am small
So I suppose I'll never be tall.
My cousin is seven
She towers over me.
I'm eleven, and smaller you see.
My brown eyes shine
I have hair so fine.
I am tiny and neat
And my mum says very sweet,
But I wish I was tall
Not petite and so small.

Sara Rainey (11)
St Joseph's Cathedral School

ALONE IN THE MOONLIGHT

Alone in the moonlight
The moon looks like a hole in the sky
That lets light come through
It moves across the sky like a boat
Gently sailing in the sea
In the moonlit garden I can see scary trees
That seem to reach out to me
The shadows look almost alive
They are so scary
I feel too scared to even tremble.

Bethan John (9)
St Joseph's Cathedral School

FRAGMENTED POEM

I am the beach
The sand is soft and sparkling in the sun.
Cold when covered with water from the waves.

I am the wave I crash into rocks.
I am dark blue and deep,
I splash against the cliffs.
I am the cliffs, full of cracks,
Birds build their nests in me, lay their eggs.
I am grey and green. At the top of me
There is a church.

I am the church with a tall steeple,
People come and pray in me.
Stained glass windows let in coloured light
Hear my bell ring.

Sarah Powell (11)
St Joseph's Cathedral School

FEAR IS . . .

Fear is like a black monster,
It tastes like a mouthful of beetles,
And smells like smoke,
And sounds like a jet's engine flying,
Fear is like a black room with no windows or doors.

Scott Clark (10)
St Joseph's Cathedral School

FRAGMENTED POETRY

I am the village with lots of shops.
In the shops the shopkeeper sells whatever
he can.
I am dusty but clean with bins around.
The sounds are residents talking.

I am a resident, finely dressed.
I go to shops, spend lots of money.
I throw chocolate wrappers into the bin.

I am a bin, horrible and smelly.
I have a sticker saying *'Clean our village'* on me.

I am a shopkeeper who sells lots of sweets
and chocolate cakes.

I make chocolate cakes.
Sometimes I fill my mug with melted
chocolate.

Rory Oldroyd (10)
St Joseph's Cathedral School

ALONE IN THE MOONLIGHT

Alone in the moonlight
It shines on me like a candle that's burning
It moves like a ghost
Across the dark starry sky

I see a peach glowing gold and red
Shadows are everywhere
Huge and small
I hear trees rustling and the wind gliding
Through the sky
I feel scared
I shiver and hide behind the bushes.

Joanna Parsonage (8)
St Joseph's Cathedral School

WHAT COULD WE SEE?

We could see a posing, purring, polar bear
With hilarious, horrible hair
It may growl a gruffy, grumbling growl
As it lets out a hideous, hasty howl.

We could see the pointy, princely pyramids
Standing under the sunny, sizzling sun
Along came the chomping, cantering camels
Having fabulous, frenzied fun.

We could see the Alps
Covered in silky, shivering snow
Children building silly, slippery snowmen
All in a row
Skiers skiing on a slippery, slidy slope
Clinging on to a rough, ragged rope.

Michelle Romano (8)
St Joseph's Cathedral School

WHAT I HAVE EATEN

I have eaten some strawberry jelly
Which slithered into my belly
I have eaten some mushy peas
With some savoury faggots if you please

I have eaten some lovely roast Welsh lamb
Followed by rice pudding and jam
I have eaten some chocolate fudge cake
Which was easy to bake.

Rebecca James (9)
St Joseph's Cathedral School

INSIDE THE BAG

Inside the bag
Was a little white spotted Dalmatian
For him to love

Inside the bag
Was a scrumptious, gigantic turkey dinner
For him to eat

Inside the bag
Was a picture of all his friends playing on the beach
For him to look at when he was lonely

Inside the bag
Was a letter
For him to remember
How his parents used to feel about him.

Daniel Jones (8)
St Joseph's Cathedral School

INSIDE THE BAG

Inside the bag
Was a little surprise
A little toy
To cheer him up

Inside the bag
Was some dinner for him
A big turkey meal
For him to eat

Inside the bag
Was a little puppy
Brown with white spots
For him to play with

Inside the bag
Was a friendly robot
That looked like him
So it would do his work
So he could play

Inside the bag
Was a cute loveable teddy
To cheer him up

Inside the bag
Was a picture of his parents
To remind him of them.

Christopher McCarley (8)
St Joseph's Cathedral School

FOODS

Chocolate is lovely
Chocolate is sweet
Chocolate makes me happy
It's my favourite thing to eat

Sprouts are horrible
Sprouts taste bad
They're a yucky green vegetable
To eat them makes me sad

Chips are great
When dipped in red sauce
Piled high on my plate
I eat them like a horse.

Cathal O'Connor (8)
St Joseph's Cathedral School

SPACE PLAY

The moonlight shining brightly on the house,
As quiet as a mouse,
The children cuddle their teddies,
And play around with Saturn's hat,
The morning arises the day goes by,
The sun comes up and says hi.

We spring up into space,
And see Jupiter's face,
Pluto sleeps above in space,
And maybe has a human race,
The stars twinkle in the sky,
As the night goes dancing by.
Venus hot, hot as burning fire,
While Pluto orbits and never tires.

Jessica Kennedy (9)
St Joseph's Cathedral School

ALONE IN THE MOONLIGHT

Alone in the moonlight
The moon shines like a torch
It goes through the sky
Like a ship on a gentle sea
It moves through the sky
Like an eagle gliding
Clouds move gently in the breeze
In the moonlit garden all you can see
are creepy shadows
Scary, tall and moving in the breeze
The wind howling through the trees
I feel like someone in another world.

Daniel Richards (9)
St Joseph's Cathedral School

I'LL TELL YOU WHAT FRIGHTENS ME . . .

I'll tell you what frightens me, spiders,
Spiders that eat you,
I'll tell you what frightens me, vertigo
It goes so high
I'll tell you what frightens me, shadows
Shadows that follow you in the dark
I'll tell you what frightens me, thunder
Thunder that thumps day or night
That's what frightens me.

I'll tell you what frightens me, guns,
Guns banging all around,
I'll tell you what frightens me, tidal waves,
Flooding the city and nowhere to escape.
I'll tell you what frightens me, nightmares,
Scary ones so you can't go back to sleep.
I'll tell you what frightens me, war,
Shooting and dying a waste of lives.

Peter Hinder (10)
St Joseph's Cathedral School

THE FIGHT

The fight - frightened
Want to run away, fast
Tears in my eyes
Fists flying blood dripping
It's a loser's game.

Lee Boland (9)
St Joseph's Cathedral School

SECRET OF THE NIGHT

Far beyond the stars,
The moon brightly shines,
Like silver skin,
Sometimes like a single gold star,
Faint at first,
And as pure as a lemon.

The moon suspended into space,
Sometimes there,
Sometimes not,
Sometimes fat,
Sometimes thin,
Night after night,
With its pale silver skin.

Liam Nolan (10)
St Joseph's Cathedral School

SPACE WALTZ

The moon is like a silver star,
Shining silently in the night,
Slowly beams of silvery gleam,
Shines upon mother nature,
And shines upon the horizon.

Scampering out of the atmosphere,
Dancing through the solar system,
Motionless the moon shines brightly,
All the night through.

James Evans (10)
St Joseph's Cathedral School

THE FIGHT

The fight began with a worried bash,
All I could hear was crash, crash, crash.
I wanted to surrender, give it all up,
Or fight like a lion or run like a scared little pup.

I ran like the wind,
As quick as a flash,
But all I could think of,
Was that I should dash.

The first blow was solid,
It stung like a bee,
The afternoon went dark,
I could barely see.

The people were cheering,
Like in a football match,
But if he was a fisherman,
I'd be a trembling catch.

James Steward (9)
St Joseph's Cathedral School

THE FIGHT

Sick and scared
Clenched fists coming towards me
As fast as bullets,
Numb in the stomach,

My legs like jelly,
My nose like a scarlet fountain,
Blood dripping all over the sidewalk,
I try to run but my legs are too stiff,

A cloudless sky,
A carless road,
Deserted street,
And it seemed no one was there
Just me and him,

I had new body parts;
Jelly for legs,
My nose a red fountain,
And now I have no stomach.

Carlie Norman (9)
St Joseph's Cathedral School

I'll Tell You What Frightens Me

I'll tell you what frightens me, vertigo,
Vertigo swings so high and feels like you are
going to fall down . . . down . . . down.
I'll tell you what frightens me, tarantulas,
When they crawl up your arm with their poisonous bite.
I'll tell you what frightens me, guns,
Guns when they sound so close the gunshot will hit you.
I'll tell you what frightens me, volcanoes,
Volcanoes that erupt and the lava chases me,
That's what frightens me.
I'll tell you what frightens me, lightning,
Lightning that sounds like it's going to hit your roof.
I'll tell you what frightens me, tornadoes,
When they pull up houses and drop them somewhere else.

Nicholas Morris (9)
St Joseph's Cathedral School

I'LL TELL YOU WHAT FRIGHTENS ME . . .

I'll tell you what frightens me, sharks,
Sharks that have sharp teeth.

I'll tell you what frightens me, war,
War that has spitfires.

I'll tell you what frightens me, water,
Water that is hot and burns.

I'll tell you what frightens me, horror books,
Horror books that have monsters.

I'll tell you what frightens me, bombs,
Bombs that fall on you and kill.

I'll tell you what frightens me, tornadoes,
Tornadoes that spin round and round.

I'll tell you what frightens me, ghosts,
Ghosts that hover above.

That's what frightens me.

Nicholas Stevens (9)
St Joseph's Cathedral School

ORBS IN SPACE

Space, big and black,
The Earth is coming back,
To its night position,
Space program astronauts,
Just landed on the moon.

The sun hot, hot as lava,
The Earth a green and blue orb,
Swimming across a vast black sea,
An amazing planet that holds you and me.

Aaron Davies (9)
St Joseph's Cathedral School

I'LL TELL YOU WHAT FRIGHTENS ME

I'll tell you what frightens me, illness,
Illness frightens me because my mind
plays tricks on me.

I'll tell you what frightens me, falling,
Thinking of falling off a cliff.

I'll tell you what frightens me, horror films,
Very scary horror films.

I'll tell you what frightens me, illness,
Illness frightens me because my mind
plays tricks on me.

I'll tell you what frightens me, falling,
Think of falling off a cliff.

I'll tell you what frightens me, horror films,
Very scary horror films.

That's what frightens me!

Michael McGrotty (9)
St Joseph's Cathedral School

I'LL TELL YOU WHAT FRIGHTENS ME

I'll tell you what frightens me, spiders
Spiders are hairy and horrible.

I'll tell you what frightens me, the dark
In the dark I think someone is going to get me.

I'll tell you what frightens me, jellyfish
Jellyfish are slimy and can sting you.

I'll tell you what frightens me, bees
Bees can sting you.

That's what frightens me.

Natalie Davies (9)
St Joseph's Cathedral School

THE FIGHT

When the fight begins scared and worried,
Like the world's caving in,
Street deserted, carless road all lonely,
My knees are banging.

You cannot hear a pin drop,
Face to face with Marv,
Wish Ezzie was here,
Try to run but nowhere to go.

Feel sick, stiff, slow,
Eyes with fire in them,
I want to go home,
Wish someone was watching.

I am not going to look anymore,
Cloudless in the sky,
Rough punches in my face,
I wish I did not write on walls now.

Samantha Ahern (9)
St Joseph's Cathedral School

THE SEASIDE

I am the bright yellow beach,
that the cold blue and green
waves weave over me from the rolling sea,

I am the sea that people jump in,
the gulls put their beaks in me,

I am the gulls that dip in the sea,
cold and bitter, blue waves turning,

I am the blue waves turning over and over,
the sun shines on me and makes me glow,

I am the sun that makes the sea glow,
I am really hot sometimes,
I go behind the clouds,

I am the clouds that cover the sun,
so people won't get sunburnt.

Rebecca Donovan (11)
St Joseph's Cathedral School

THE FIGHT

Sick, dangerous, hateful
Punches, sound like smashing cars
Daring, 90% sure hammerman will win
In my eyes are watery tears

One punch in the stomach then another
Stomach is hurting
He will keep on doing it and doing it
Again and again.

Kurt Velardo (9)
St Joseph's Cathedral School

I'LL TELL YOU WHAT FRIGHTENS ME . . .

I'll tell you what frightens me, a hole in the ozone,
A hole in the ozone will cause skin disease.
I'll tell you what frightens me, engine failure,
Engine failure making planes crash.
I'll tell you what frightens me, meteorites,
Meteorites that smash when they hit the ground.
I'll tell you what frightens me, footsteps
Footsteps from the darkness, and you don't know who they belong to.
That's what frightens me!

Joseph Parkhouse (9)
St Joseph's Cathedral School

FEAR IS . . .

Fear is black as black as my pen,
It tastes like sour milk,
It smells like stale cheese,
It looks like a fearless soldier,
It sounds like my teacher moaning at me,
Fear is me!

Gary MacMullen (10)
St Joseph's Cathedral School

I AM THE WORLD

I am the world, I see beautiful green meadows
And wonderful stars at night that are fantastic
Glow of the sun in the sky at morning means
That my beautiful flowers can grow
But also when I get angry erupt my volcanoes

I am the volcano, my lava kills
And destroys everything that is in my path
It is red and hot and pours into the sea

I am the sea I know all the fishes and sharks
That live in me, I crash against the rocks
Some are small rocks and some are big rocks

I am the rocks I have watched everything
That has come and gone well before anyone
Made man

I am the man I live in this world I watch
The grass grow volcanoes erupt and the
Sea that crashes against the rocks.

Bethan Michelle Flavin (11)
St Joseph's Cathedral School

AUTUMN POEM

Autumn is here, leaves
turn brown, squirrels come
out to run around, hedgehogs
go snuffle in the dry leaves,
birds fly away from the trees.

Freya Thobroe (9)
St Joseph's RC Primary School, Clydach

DREAMING

Grooming, brushing around and around,
Combing his tail which is down to the ground.
Giving him an apple for standing still,
Getting him to sparkle so he can win,
Walking around, go into a trot,
He is so sweet as he plods along,
Into a canter, are we over the jump?
Of course we are, let's jump, jump, jump.
Over the second over the third,
I am wearing my lucky brooch-bird.
When the class finished they called out the winner,
Come on Dinky, I hope we're a killer,
Third! Second! First! It's us!
Oh! Look at that girl she's making such a fuss.
Look at our rosette big and bright,
I bet it's shinier in the light,
I'm so happy, I'll stick it on the wall,
'It's teatime,' my mother calls,
It's nice to dream, I suppose.

Ffion Cooke (9)
St Joseph's RC Primary School, Clydach

BLUE

Blue is the colour
of sea
and sky
my favourite colour
yours too
but it's cold
Who cares?
Not I
not you.

Juliette Harris (10)
St Joseph's RC Primary School, Clydach

SPRING

The green leaves come alive on the bush
'Goodbye' says the robin, 'Hello,' says the thrush
Daffodils and primroses are yellow bright
But the gentle snowdrop remains snow-white
The lambs skip round, a pretty sight
The longer the day the shorter the night
The sun comes out from behind the horizon
All the children pray
That winter's gone for another year
And summer's on its way.

Gabrielle Barrett (10)
St Joseph's RC Primary School, Clydach

I IMAGINE

I imagine that I am a
sailor,
Sailing through the roaring seas.

I imagine that I am a
pilot,
Flying through the bright blue
skies.

I imagine that I am a train
driver,
Driving through the hills and
valleys.

I imagine that I am a bus
driver,
Driving through the busy
streets.

But best of all I like to be, *me* -
A boy who is happy as can be.

Kurien Parel (10)
St Joseph's RC Primary School, Clydach

HOMEWORK

Homework's boring, it's no fun,
When you want to be playing out in the sun.
My friends are waiting for me up at the park,
But I'm stuck with my homework until dark.

When I finish my homework I dread the Friday that week,
Science, arithmetic, what else could there be?
I think of my friends racing on ahead.
I'll probably do homework until I'm dead!

Catherine Morgan (9)
St Joseph's RC Primary School, Clydach

WOULDN'T IT BE . . .

Wouldn't it be cool if you could
go to the moon.
Wouldn't it be good if the Spice Girls
came to town.
Wouldn't it be cool if you had
ten legs and six heads
Wouldn't it be good if you could
eat one million Easter eggs
Wouldn't it be radical if school got
blown up.
Wouldn't it be cool if school definitely
did get blown up 'Way cool.'
Wouldn't it be cool if you went on a
jungle hike.
Wouldn't it be cool if you had a dog
called Spike.
Wouldn't it be cool if we were
made of slime,
And that's the end of my rhyme.

Erika Butler (9)
St Joseph's RC Primary School, Clydach

ANIMALS ANIMALS

Animals usually feel like silk
Cats usually like drinking milk
Dogs lick and bark like mad
And sometimes annoy my mum and dad
You have to love them
They're as valuable as a crystal gem
They run around the trees
And try to eat the bees
I really can't help loving them all
The way they eat and chase a ball.

Hayley Codd (10)
St Joseph's RC Primary School, Clydach

TREES

Trees come in all shapes and sizes
They come big and small
They come in all different colours
Depending on the time of year
All their leaves are different
Some spiky, some curled, some round
And if you sometimes go out in the woods
Often they are round.

Michaela Jones (10)
St Joseph's RC Primary School, Clydach

LIVING THINGS

Look out of my window
See butterflies
Look out of my window
Have a big surprise
Look out of my window
See the forest
Look at the foxes running
Look out of my window
I can see my horses
King, Magic, Flash and Sunshine
Running in the field as they wish
Look out of my window
My cat's playing in the garden
Look out of my window
See my dogs chasing one another
Turn around I can see the fish
On my wall
Go downstairs I can see real fish
Going round and round the tank
Go into my lounge
The TV is on *Hey Arnold*
Hooray!

Victoria Jones (10)
St Joseph's RC Primary School, Clydach

HOUSES

Houses are very large and tall
Sometimes they can be so small
They're built in all different sizes and shapes
With many windows and garden gates,
Some have gardens with many flowers
Where in the summer we like to sit for hours and hours
In the kitchen we do the cooking
Making many dinners and scrumptious puddings,
In the living room we watch television and relax
Where many dads watch a football match
The bedroom is where we go to sleep
To dream about memories we like to keep,
At the end of the day houses are quiet and still
Until dawn breaks when birds begin to sing on my window-sill.

Natalie Johnson (9)
St Joseph's RC Primary School, Clydach

MY MUM

My mum is kind,
My mum is nice,
My mum cares for me,
My mum is good,
My mum is bad,
But still she cares for me

My mum she is a dentist,
She works in Ystradgynlais,
She has curly hair, and she looks very nice,
She loves me and my brother and sister,
And she also loves my dad,
But she doesn't love me most,
She loves us all the same.

Gina Earland (9)
St Joseph's RC Primary School, Clydach

MY DAD

My dad is a doctor,
They call him Doctor Lloyd.
And sometimes when we are naughty,
He really gets annoyed.

He splits up me and my sisters,
On different chairs or spots,
He drives us up to hospital,
When we get chickenpox.

But he really is very kind,
He takes us out on bikes,
And when he wakes up in the morning,
His hair is all in spikes.

Jennifer Lloyd (9)
St Joseph's RC Primary School, Clydach

PEOPLE

People are kind,
People are sad,
People are good,
People are bad,
People help
People care
I like people everywhere!

People are busy,
Some at bus-stops,
People are rushing
Going into shops
People care,
People, people everywhere!

Some people are busy
And have to work
Some are gentle
Some are caring
Most care and help
But my mother helps me most.

Fiona Ryan (9)
St Joseph's RC Primary School, Clydach

SWANSEA BAY

I cross the bridge by the old Saint Helen's baths,
I look forward to a day of sunshine and laughs.
The last of Joe's ice-cream melting in my hand.
For miles all I can see is golden yellow sand.
I can hear the seagulls calling above my head.
I can hear the waves crashing against the sea bed.
I take in a deep breath of the salty sea air,
And see an old lady snoozing on a deck-chair.
Sandcastles with flags that flutter in the breeze.
Sand blown up my nose that makes me sneeze.
A baby grizzles and is picked up by its Mum.
An old man snores on a towel, his legs reddened by the sun.
I put on my sun hat against the sun's glare.
I stroll along the beach towards the funfair.
On the old Swansea rec I hear teenagers squeal,
They're stuck at the top of the funfair's big wheel.
I'm tired now, it's time I should stop
I open my bag, eat my pastie, crisps and pop.
The sun starts to set, over a busy Mumbles Bay.
It's time to pack up, head home after a wonderful day.

Heather Tucker (11)
Terrace Road Primary School, Swansea

LLANDUDNO BAY

Sh . . .sh . . .sh . . . whispers the sea, as it laps onto the golden shore.
Eek, eek, screech the hungry seagulls,
       as they fly around, scavenging for food.
Ee-or, squeals a donkey, as a young girl climbs on its saddle.
Crunch! A few cockle shells smash,
       as a giant beach ball bounces off them.
'Uuh,' sighs an old man, as he plonks himself on a deck-chair.
'One-nil, one-nil,' exclaims a teenage boy,
       who has heard the full-time football whistle.
'Hooray!' cheers the winner of the sandcastle competition,
       as he collects his prize.
Bleep, bleep, chirps the metal detector,
       as it hits an old tin can embedded in the sand.
'Arrh . . . vacancies!' beams a hotel hunting family.
'Jackpot!' comes the cry from the amusement arcade,
       as the machine tumbles out money.
'Hold tight!' implores the simulator as the doors slam shut.
'Eeey-aaaah' scream the people on the roller-coaster,
       as they wave their hands in the air.
'Llandudno postcards for one and all,'
       bellows the owner of a souvenir shop.
Slam, go the shutters, as everything comes to a close.
The only sound now is snoring!

Lucie Barron (11)
Terrace Road Primary School, Swansea

HAMSTER

My hamster is a worry
she runs around in a hurry
she lives in a house
with room for a mouse

She runs miles in her wheel
but I never hear her squeal
I give her a choc drop
that never makes her stop

She sleeps by day
I wish she would play
by night she plays
while I am away

In my bed I sleep
I wish I could go down and peep
but with school in the morning
the day is dawning

Truffle is her name
she likes playing a game
she has a cute face
but can be a disgrace

I love her to pieces
she tickles our faces
I am so glad to have her
and to tickle her fur.

Samantha Ace (10)
Tre-Gwyr Junior School

WEATHER

Weather is gentle weather is strong
When the wind blows it's a real storm
You'd wish it was summer
When the sun makes us warm

Weather is kind the weather is wild
Down comes the rain to make us all wet
No going out to play
Indoors all day I bet

Weather is icy weather is cold
Down comes the snow and makes it all white
Wrap up warm out we go
To have a snowball fight

The weather is unpredictable
You never know what it will bring
In summer and autumn
And winter and spring

Scott Daniel McCoubrey (9)
Tre-Gwyr Junior School

MY DOG

I once had a dog called Bess
who often made a mess.
She would run around
chasing a pound
wagging her tail behind her.
With her jet-black hair
and her floppy ears
it was a delight to have loved her.

Now all I have is memories of her,
a photo by my bed.
Never mind. I now have a big ted
who shares my bed,
now Bess has gone
life still goes on, she's
always in my head.

Sarah Ace (10)
Tre-Gwyr Junior School

OUR TRIP

Early start, don't lose your rag
Hurry up and pack your bag
We're going on a trip to Spain
On the biggest ever aeroplane

It flies at ninety miles an hour
With a hundred and forty horse power
It take up over twenty crew
With big huge windows you get a view

Now we've reached our destination
It's sun and sea and meditation
Why not have a look in the shops
To buy our friends some lollipops

Jonathan Lewis (9)
Tre-Gwyr Junior School

THE ZOO IN MY PENCIL CASE

My rubber is a rhino,
Scrambling across my work,
Rubbing out the words which are wrong.
My pencil is a snake,
Slithering across the words,
Hissing at the ones which are wrong.
My protractor is a hedgehog,
With its spikes going in all angles.
My fountain pen is a mum stick insect helping
My cartridge which is a baby stick insect write on my paper.
My pen is the zoo keeper,
Guiding the animals to work out sums and write stories on my paper.

Lucy Chieffo (11)
Tre-Gwyr Junior School

ONE DAY ON ST DAVID'S DAY

One day on March the first we celebrate St David's birth
We wear our costumes, daffodils and leeks
To sing songs we have been practising for weeks.

The brownies are going to St John's church with Brown Owl,
Then home again for Welsh cakes and cawl.

We have twmpath dancing and in Eisteddfodau we sing
In black hats and shawl, hoping it's pleasure we bring.
To teachers and pupils who watch us perform
To commemorate the day St David was born.

Rebecca Johns (9)
Tre-Gwyr Junior School

POEM FOR A HOUSE

Houses are big, houses are small,
Houses are wide, houses are tall,
Houses have flowers, houses have grass,
Houses have a pathway, to let people pass,
Houses have chimneys, houses have a roof,
Houses have windows wherever you move.

Houses come in all shapes and designs,
Bungalows, terraces, whatever the size,
Houses have attics, houses have rooms,
Houses have kitchens where you keep all the brooms,
Houses have roofs, brown roofs and red,
Houses have curtains, if you peep in, there's a bed,
Houses have gardens, houses have a fence,
Houses might have a sign which says they're up for rent.

Houses have bricks, houses have mortar
Houses have gutters, that run down with water
Houses have heating, houses have rafters,
Houses have a dining-room with main meal and afters,
Houses have building companies, Cymric and Barratts.
Houses have cages for canaries and parrots,
Houses have sinks, houses have a bath,
Houses have a hall to make a clear path.

Houses have radiators and bathroom tiles,
Houses have a study with books and files,
Houses have a staircase that goes round and round,
Houses have mice which don't make a sound,
Houses have chairs that go back far,
Outside the house you will find a parked car,
Houses have garages, houses have a porch,
And up in the attic you need a bright torch.

David King (9)
Tre-Gwyr Junior School

FEELINGS

I wish my grandfather was here,
To sit beside him and feel so safe.
To tell me about his life.
I wish he was still here,
It was the best time in the world.
When my brave, strong grandfather was alive.
It was the happiest time of my life.
My grandfather was the best the Lord could pick.
I am the luckiest boy in the world,
I feel sad that my grandfather has gone.
I feel as lonely as could be.
I feel I want to die to join him up in the sky.
I don't know why he has gone.

Damion Williams (10)
Tre-Gwyr Junior School

I REMEMBER

I remember when Mum called us down.
She told us Grandad had an accident.
I remember when my uncle rang.
And told us what had happened.

I remember when my uncle rang again.
He said he had hypothermia,
I remember he said he was on a big machine.
To help him stay alive.

I remember the next morning, when Mum woke us up.
Then we went downstairs.
We went to school and then came home.
And Mum nodded her head.

I knew what she was saying.
I knew that he was dead.
My brother was upstairs sulking
But he didn't really care.

Amira Bond (10)
Tre-Gwyr Junior School

CRY FOR FREEDOM

China, India, Africa,
Are to name but three,
From wood carvings and clothing,
To picking our favourite tea.

When will they have time to play,
When will they have time to learn?
This issue is bigger
Than the coppers they earn.

Come on people around the world,
Allow them to play -
Before they're too old,
End child labour!

Alyx Williams (11)
Tre-Gwyr Junior School

THE ZOO IN MY PENCIL CASE

There is a zoo in my pencil case,
Pull back the zip and see,
My pens standing tall together, giraffes eating from a tree.
My eraser is a hungry hippo eating up the words
My fountain pen is an eagle in charge of all the birds.
My compass is a flamingo standing on one leg,
Scissors snapping, a crocodile making everyone feel scared
Peep into my pencil case and take a look and see,
The sharpened bits they rest upon,
Smell like shavings off a tree.

Charlotte Miles (10)
Tre-Gwyr Junior School

FREEDOM

I think that this is very bad,
Actually I think that it is mad,
Children working in factories,
Making money for their families.

Slaving all day as the sun beats down,
With faces so sad and tears and frown,
Fingers are aching and eyes are sore,
As they sit at their machines and work
More, more, more.

Although I live far away from there,
I know that it must be tough,
And very hard to bear.
I hope that child labour all soon ends,
So that they can go to school,
And make some new friends.

Rhian Bateman (10)
Tre-Gwyr Junior School

SNOW

I love it when it starts to snow
The world is clear and bright
It's fun to play with in the day
And nice to watch at night.

It makes your fingers feel so cold
But still it's nice to touch
Building snowmen, throwing balls
I love it oh so much.

It falls from the sky upon your head
It makes your hair all white
It makes your toes and fingers tingle
Your red nose glows so bright.

Emma Thomas (10)
Tre-Gwyr Junior School

SUNNING

Old dog lay in summer sun
Much too lazy to rise and run
He flapped an ear on a buzzing fly
He winked a half opened sleepy eye
He scratched himself on an itching spot
He dozed on the porch when the sun was hot.
He whimpered a bit from force of habit
While he lazily dreamed of chasing a rabbit
But old dog happily lay in the sun
Much too lazy to rise and run

Christopher Williams (10)
Tre-Gwyr Junior School

TIME TRAVEL

I know an old man called Mr Past,
He likes travelling through time,
He likes travelling fast,
I like Mr Past, he's a good friend of mine.

I know an old man called Mr Present,
He stays where he is,
At home with his pheasants,
I like Mr Present, he's a good friend of mine.

I know an old man called Mr Future,
He travels through time,
He travels on a hoover,
I like Mr Future, he's a good friend of mine.

Dawn Elizabeth Emmerton (10)
Tre-Gwyr Junior School

POETRY IS TOO HARD

Poetry, poetry
Is too hard for me;
I will not admit defeat;
So instead I'll have to cheat.

I will copy someone's rhyme;
And pretend that it is mine;
Mr Casey will find out;
And for that I'll have a clout.

So instead I'll write my own;
In front of the class it shall be shown;
And against my premonition;
I might win the competition.

Leigh Jago (9)
Tre-Gwyr Junior School

THE STORM

Wind whistling under the door, blowing tiles off the roof.
Doors banging, shaking the frames.
Windows rattling, while draughts blow making me shiver,
Cold to the bone.
Thunder shaking the house, growing louder and louder.
Clouds moving faster, pelting down the powerful rain.
Trees snapping and twigs being pulled by wind into the distance.
The biggest storm ever.

Adam Vaughan (10)
Waunarlwydd Primary School

THE STORM

Waves crashing and smashing against the rocks,
Wind screaming and howling,
Thunder booming and drumming, getting closer and closer,
Waves cave in, causing ships to crash into rocks and sink,
Rain like a waterfall right above,
Dark clouds start to crawl across the dark sky,
It's very cold now as the water splashes.
It's frightening out there.

Gavin Morgan (10)
Waunarlwydd Primary School

STORM

I lay in my bed curled up in my quilt,
Listen to the gentle tap of water.
Suddenly the tree knocks at the window.
I jump in terror!
I hear the tiles flap like a bird taking off.
My dog barks at the shed door
Banging against the wooden frame.
My pets stay unseen until the storm is over.
The lights flicker wildly,
Leaving us in darkness for seconds.
I sleep under my bed -it is quiet there.
A chill creeps down my spine.
The thunder rolls through the sky
Like a bowling ball and cracks above.

Christopher Lazell (11)
Waunarlwydd Primary School

THE RAIN

I live in the clouds, which gracefully float around the world.
The oceans and the rivers are my brothers.
My sisters are the dew on a summer's morning
and the first frost on a winter's night.
I have two deadly enemies, the blazing hot sun and
the speedy transparent wind.
I eat everything in my path that is dry then swallow
it whole, leaving it dripping wet.
My favourite colour is royal blue because it represents
my friends and I.
I go around the world drenching everything I see and meet.

Amy Ross (11)
Waunarlwydd Primary School

THE WIND

I can howl like a wolf in the night.
I live where no one else knows.
I creep up on unsuspecting victims,
And cause mischief wherever I go.
My relations are many,
Including the tornado,
The breeze and the air.
I take people's washing,
And blow it away.
I enjoy it on wash day,
When I can go out to play.
I can go fast and also slow,
I can go high and then very low.
People call me the *wind.*

Geraint Probert (10)
Waunarlwydd Primary School

THE STORM

The wind was howling,
Like a wolf on a cold, wet night.
The rain boomed against the walls,
As if there was no way out.
The thunder rumbled and crashed,
As if it were guarding the night sky.
The waves seemed alive,
Jumping and spitting everywhere.
The stars and moon had been overtaken
By dark clouds.
The storm had begun.

David Berry (10)
Waunarlwydd Primary School

THE WIND

Wind, wind, why do you cry,
And why do you sing nasty lullabies?

I am the king of the rain and the hail,
Can't you tell by their colours so pale.
My colour is blue, white and grey.
The storm is my best friend, he's just the same.
Have you seen the magic colours the storm leaves behind?
The purple, the pink, grey and blue.
They are so different, but they don't suit you.

Wind, wind, what be your name?
You can tell me, I'm not afraid.

Cheerful, cheerful is my name,
For I do not moan, although I am as cold as stone.
Now you must go, I won't keep your time,
For I see the clouds are chancing to change.

Sarah Miller (11)
Waunarlwydd Primary School

THE TWISTER

I am the twister, rough and tumble,
I live wherever I can,
In the rivers, the seas, the oceans, the quays,
I swirl around like a fan.

My enemy is the deadly sun,
As yellow as a bale of hay,
He sits there laughing in the west or the east,
And always comes out to play.

I am as old as the end of time,
And come along with the deadliest chime,
Into the mountains and hills I climb,
    For I am the deadly twister.

Thomas Stephens (11)
Waunarlwydd Primary School

MY ALIEN

The alien from my planet
Is smellier than a skunk
As cool as some ice-cream
Has hair like a punk

As funny as a puppet
As thin as a pin
As deadly as a bee
As nasty as a sting

The alien from my planet
Is smellier than a rat
As sludgy as a swamp
But he's as daft as a bat

Sam Bevan (9)
Ynystawe Primary School

MY ALIEN

The alien from my planet
Is friendlier than a dog
As fast as a horse
As beautiful as a frog
As busy as a bee
As pink as a rose
As bright as the sun
As tickly as toes.

As happy as can be
As clever as a fox
As healthy as a fruit
As cunning as an ox
The alien from my planet
Is smarter than a teacher
As fat as a pig
But not a very good preacher

Elizabeth Chambers (9)
Ynystawe Primary School

MY ALIEN

The alien from Mars,
Is nuttier than a fruit cake,
As fat as a turkey,
As slimy as a snake.

As wide as a school,
As smelly as a skunk.
As wet as a swimming pool,
As weak as a monk.

The alien from Mars,
Is rounder than a ball,
As hairy as a fairy,
But not scary at all.

Sam Barrett (9)
Ynystawe Primary School

MY ALIEN

The alien from my planet,
Is as green as peas,
As scary as a tiger
But is as busy as bees.

The alien from my planet
Is as fat as a pig
As short as a gnome,
As shy as a horse,
As spiky as a comb.

But when he runs he looks like jelly
He's as impatient as a baby
He wiggles his belly.

Delyth Morris (10)
Ynystawe Primary School

ME AND YOU

Planets, stars, comets,
Craters, sunsets, boulders too.
Amazing sights for me and you.

Silent stars,
Spacious universe with planets too,
Gleaming meteors and UFOs
Amazing sights for me and you.

Cosmic adventure
A black hole or two,
Amazing sights for me and you.

Jason Williams (11)
Ysgol Gymraeg Ynysgedwyn

WHAT'S IN SPACE?

What's in space?
Planets like Jupiter
As warm as amber.
Cold Pluto, as small as a
Piece of glitter thrown
To the end of the universe.

What's in space?
Spaceships like
Spinning silver
Saucers without
A cup or spoon.

What's in space?
Stars like big
Blobs of gold paint,
Spilt from an artist's palette into the darkness,
And rockets whizzing,
Like javelins thrown from
Earth.

What's in space?
The moon so bright,
Feather light,
And looks like Earth but
Yet so cold and starry bold.

That's what's in space!

Catrin James (10)
Ysgol Gymraeg Ynysgedwyn

ALIENS? I DON'T THINK SO!

Aliens in space?
Who would have thought?
If there were aliens in space they would
have been caught!

All the people who have gone *up there*
Say they've never seen anything, not
anywhere.

High above the sparkly stars,
Could there be aliens living on Mars?
Surely not, they'd have no air,
Not amongst the stars up there.

Everyone says they do not exist.
I've thought about this for, oh, so long.
There are *no* aliens up there.
Aaaarrrggghhh!

I guess I was wrong!

Lowri Evans (10)
Ysgol Gymraeg Ynysgedwyn

COSMIC

Have you ever wondered what there is to know,
About the universe and its mysterious glow?
The gassy balls that we call stars,
Just appear like gleaming jars!
And what about aliens, do they come with heads?
If so, are they made of lead, garden sheds,
Or maybe a chimney instead!
Do they have *stupendous* brains,
Or are they simply the size of bread grains?
Maybe . . . they cook you by the sun,
Until you are fully *done!*
Or . . . maybe they're like a baby toy,
Leaping around so full of joy!
The powdery moon like a giant golf ball,
To some gardeners the surface would appal!
Yes, there's a *lot* we don't know about that
Weird and wonderful place, but if it were food,
It would have a very beautiful taste!

Alex Glendenning (11)
Ysgol Gymraeg Ynysgedwyn

COSMOS

C is for comets floating in space
O is for open world, a huge and glittery place
S is for stars you feel like catching in jars
M is for Martians floating around stars
O is for orbit circling so free
S is for sparkling universe a wonderful place to be

Holly Best (10)
Ysgol Gymraeg Ynysgedwyn

THE COSMIC MOON

The moon does shine,
High above,
Floating above,
So dead and creepy!

Planets like puppets on a string,
Spinning round and round,
365 days a year,
All round and misty.

Shooting stars,
Flying saucers,
Little green men,
All bubbly and bouncy,
Jumping out from craters.

Glistening stars,
Floating above our heads,
Oh how cool to float to Mars,
Flying around and dancing free,
Oh how cool it would be!

Bethan Morgan (11)
Ysgol Gymraeg Ynysgedwyn